YOUR THOUGHTS ARE KILLING YOU

TAKE CONTROL OF YOUR MIND AND CLOSE
THE DOOR TO DEPRESSION, ANXIETY AND
THOSE FEARFUL, WORRISOME THOUGHTS
FOREVER

MARYBETH WUENSCHEL

Spirit Filled Catholic

CONTACT ME

I want to keep in touch with you and send you inspirational emails occasionally. I would also like to send you free downloads, and I mean FREE. I won't force you to leave an email. I just want you to have them

Please Contact Me

https://www.spiritfilledcatholic.com/

https://www.spiritfilledcatholic.com/downloads

I have 12 pages of Healing Scriptures I want to get into your hands. When you are sick, or know someone who is sick, read them out loud. The Word of God is medicine and has the power to heal your whole being.

> **Proverbs 4:20-22** *My son, to my words be attentive, to my sayings incline your ear; Let them not slip from your sight, keep them within your heart; For they are life to those who find them, bringing health to one's whole being.*

Marybeth Wuenschel
mbwuenschel@gmail.com
https://www.facebook.com/catholicdevotional/

To my husband, Mark, my best friend, my confidant, my strength, and my support. I dedicate this book to you because you are the one I lean on, count on, and trust with everything I have. When I have nothing to give, you always have true love and devotion for me.

To Faith, Peter, and David, my children. I love you and thrive on your encouragement and love for me. You drive me to be more and go further. Thank you for inspiriting me to take the leap.

To my mother Pat Fischer, my biggest fan and the one who loves me unconditionally every day. Your support, friendship, and wisdom keep me engaged and on task.

To my father Raymond V. Fischer 1934-2018, the kindest and gentlest man in the world. I love you and miss you and know you would be so proud of me.

To my prayer group at St. Gabriel the Archangel Catholic Church, for your prayer support and commitment to me and to our Lord Jesus Christ.

To the one and only Father, Son, and Holy Spirit, who gave me every word and make me who I am.

1

TAKING CONTROL

I know the answer, and I cannot contain it. I want you to know that no matter what you are going through, worrying about, stressing or fretting over; no matter how long you have been feeling this way, Jesus wants you free. He wants you free from depression, worry, fear, and every thought, memory, and mood that plagues you. He has the means and the power to do it and because of Him, so do you.

I have to get the word out because I know the cure, and it works. I want this cure for you. I want you to rise up out of the pit and live a brand-new life free from every negative thought, addiction, and disease. This cure is real, it's not maybe, it's certain, and God wants you to be just as confident as I am that victory is yours.

You may feel oppressed, and you may not know why or from where it's coming. You may feel like the shoe is just about to drop. Maybe you feel impending doom or depression. YOU ARE NOT ALONE! Just hang on. Don't quit reading.

I am not suggesting to you that you quit your medicine or cancel your doctor or therapist. This book is not a replacement for your current therapy and medication. But at the same time, I can't help but offer you the best medicine out there, and it's free and comes with no side effects. Jesus doesn't have favorites. He doesn't heal some of the people some of the time. He healed them ALL, the Bible says.

> **Matthew 4:23** *"He went around all of Galilee, teaching in their synagogues, proclaiming the gospel of the kingdom, and curing every disease and illness among the people."*

> **Matthew 8:16-17** *"When it was evening, they brought Him many who were possessed by demons, and He drove out the spirits by a word and cured all the sick, to fulfill what had been said by Isaiah the prophet: 'He took away our infirmities and bore our diseases.'"*

It's your turn. You are next. Your time is now! Jesus wants to heal you and deliver you from every evil chasing you and attacking you.

The Bible says people are perishing for lack of knowledge. I am going to share some truths with you that, if you are willing to believe, will radically change your life forever so you can enjoy life and experience joy unspeakable and live a full, healthy life free of guilt and shame. Jesus said it's not the truth that sets you free but it's the knowledge of the truth that sets you free. You have the same power Jesus does because He has given it to you.

If you are open and have time for God, you will hear God's voice. Get ready to be healed, blessed, and blown away as you read through these pages. God is faithful to transform your life. He wants it for you more than you do. He did it for me and if he did it for me, he will do it for you.

I didn't deserve it. What God did for me is ridiculous. I still wonder, "Why me? How could He? Why am I so blessed?" God wants to bless you too. He wants to show off His goodness through you. Are you available? Do you want to be victorious or remain a victim? It's up to you. Do you want sympathy or victory over every area of your life? Do you feel better if you are miserable? Would you know how to handle a life free of misery? It's up to you. God has already decided He wants the good life for you. He paid a high price for you to have it. He wants peace and joy to be your norm, not something that is always just out of reach.

At 29 I was lost and didn't even know it. I hated myself and didn't know why. I just knew something was missing. I hated everything I stood for because I stood for nothing. Nothing I did ever seemed fruitful or productive or worthy of any glory. I was a coward and afraid of my own shadow. I was so afraid of what everyone else thought of me that I would never share my opinion honestly. I didn't even know I had an opinion. I was so self-conscious that my opinion changed depending on who I was with. I was shy because I was a coward and self-absorbed. I was so afraid of being wrong and exposed as a phony that I hid within myself and never shared who I really was with anyone because I was so afraid of rejection.

I wanted to be loved and respected. I wanted my life to matter. I wanted to make a difference in the world yet I was so afraid of failure I wouldn't even try. I had no respect for myself. I was a liar, a cheater, an adulterer and a murderer, yet no one knew. I was good at covering up. On the outside I was a sharp respectable business woman with an MBA. I wonder how many are just like me. How many are so empty and lost, they don't know why they are even alive? I had to be worth something. I had to have a reason to live. Everyone needs a purpose. I was about to find out just how much I was worth to God.

I want you to start living like you are a champion instead of a failure; like a winner instead of loser; alive instead of dead; and free instead of the tied up, nervous, worrisome creature that you have become or are afraid you may become. You have more authority than you know and certainly more than you are experiencing. We have more power than we understand. The Spirit that raised Jesus from the dead lives inside of you and me, the same Holy Spirit. You have the power of God in you, and you are about to unleash it. God didn't give you power so you could remain trapped and defeated.

We all have strongholds that we need to deal with or keep from developing. My desire is to help you recognize strong-holds and learn how to break their hold and demolish them. We are over-comers and perfectly equipped to gain freedom from oppression, depression, suppression, repression, and every other "...pression" you can think of.

God has given us a battle plan, and He is waiting to teach us how to fight for what is ours. The beginning of the victory and breakthrough is knowing that victory and breakthrough are yours and belong to you. The battle is fought and won by knowing who you are in Christ and what you deserve.

David fought Goliath with nothing but stones and a sling. David said to Goliath, "You come against me with sword and spear and scimitar, but I come against you in the name of the Lord of Hosts ..." David was the only one who knew who he was and what he had. The entire Israelite army was dismayed and terror-stricken when they saw Goliath. They didn't know who their God was nor what He was willing to do for them.

The weapons at our disposal are spiritual and just as powerful today against our giants as they were for David. Jesus has given us the authority and power to break free and stay free, and our freedom begins when we realize that His death on the cross did something. He set us free when He went to the cross. His death was not a normal death. It was a sacrificial death. He died for us. Freedom from negative thoughts, depression, anxiety, fear, and worry is God's desire, design, and gift to us as His children through the death of His Son.

> **THERE IS NO LIMIT** to what you can do or how far you can go. **GET READY** and prepare the cabin, put the tray tables and seats in an upright position with seat belts securely fastened, and **GET READY FOR TAKE-OFF.**

God doesn't have an ordinary, mediocre life planned for you. He doesn't have the same old, same old. He has more for you than you can think or imagine (Jeremiah 33:3).

2

STRONGHOLDS

Do your thoughts have control over you or do you have control over your thoughts? Who is in charge of your mind and your thoughts? Who decides what you think or meditate on? Who is in charge of YOU? You are about to learn that you are more than you think you are and can become more than you ever thought possible.

Do you ever let your mind wander or let your thoughts and imagination run wild? Do you like to just let your mind go and daydream? We all do at times, some like to do this more than others. We were taught that it's a good thing... "Let it go, let it go..."

Our imaginations are a good thing and a dangerous thing. God gave us imaginations so we could create, invent, play, pretend, grow, and succeed in this life. He gave us imaginations so we could dream, and wonder about Him, His creation, and His kingdom. Imaginations can work against us as well as for us. As great and wonderful as this gift is, it is very dangerous if left unattended or allowed to run wild or out of control. Imaginations are what cause a person to believe lies about themselves such as:

- "Maybe I really am perverted,"
- "Maybe I am worthless,"
- "Maybe the lady living next door really does hate me,"
- "Maybe I really would be better off dead," etc.

Do not let your mind wander. This is contrary to everything we were taught in school or growing up. We were taught to let our minds go and be creative. When our mind wanders, it is up for grabs, and the devil will take advantage. The devil will give you lots of food for thought. He loves to feed your imagination. He is relentless and merciless and will seize every opportunity to gain access, take control, and devour you. If you are not in control of your mind or imagination, the devil will be happy to do it for you.

> **Ephesians 6:16** *"Lift up the shield of faith with which you can extinguish all the flaming arrows of the evil one."*

Flaming arrows are evil thoughts. The devil is sending you evil thoughts all the time. You don't have to receive them. As a matter of fact, the more you refuse them and reject his thoughts, the sooner he will back off and quit trying. Just because thoughts come to us doesn't mean they belong to us or have to remain. There is an ongoing battle for us and a battle for our minds. The devil knows if he can get our minds, he can get us. Wickedness wants to come in, and it is always looking for an open door or an invitation. That invitation comes when we let our minds wander and think about things we know we shouldn't. What we think about matters. Jesus wants us to command our thoughts into obedience. We do not obey our thoughts; our thoughts obey us.

When we let our minds wander and continually entertain evil, negative thoughts, a stronghold develops. A stronghold is anything that has a strong hold on you. Merriam-Webster defines stronghold as: "a place dominated by a particular group or marked by a particular characteristic." In times of war you wouldn't cross certain enemy lines without a battle plan for fear you might walk into an enemy stronghold, an area or camp where the enemy is in control.

How do we recognize a stronghold and how do we get free?

A stronghold is a state of mind where you are not in complete control. Sounds heavy, but it's more common than you think. A stronghold is anything that has a tight grip on you or overwhelms you, such as feelings, emotions, habits, or sin. You want to be in control, but your emotions run away with you and carry you to where you don't want to go, such as despair or depression or fear or worry, or guilt, condemnation, or obsessive control. We say things like, "I just can't help it." When you can't help yourself and find yourself doing what you don't want to do, you are trapped in a stronghold.

When you are in a pit or depressed and can't escape or easily turn it off; this is a stronghold. A bad habit is a stronghold. Whatever has more control over you than you do over it, is a stronghold.

A stronghold begins with just a thought and, if allowed, can grow from one thought into a series of thoughts that become default thought patterns. These thoughts take control and capture what they were never authorized to take: our peace of mind and self-control.

When a thought process has a firm hold on us, then those thoughts control us because they become more powerful than our will or ability to overthrow them. We go wherever our thoughts take us. If our thoughts are left alone or left to run amuck, we will go where we never intended to go. We will become what we were never meant to become. One thought such as, "Who does he think he is?" leads to being offended or insulted, to bitterness and unforgiveness, and eventually hatred where even his or her name being mentioned triggers bad feelings and thoughts.

How do we identify a stronghold? What does it look like or feel like? We must be able to recognize negative patterns or strongholds in order to break a negative stronghold and regain control of ourselves.

The following will help you identify strongholds.

- Are you powerless to overcome and take control of your emotions?
- Are you moody and critical of others?
- Do you feel overwhelmed and
- don't know what to do first or next?
- Do you feel oppressed or depressed and don't know why or where it's coming from?
- Do you experience chronic fear or worry?
- Do you find yourself always ruining the atmosphere?
- Do your children hate to be around you?
- Are you hateful, resentful, negative, and bitter?
- Do you always seem to be angry or frustrated?

- Are you rarely satisfied, rarely content?
- Are you unsure of yourself and self-conscious?
- Are you easily offended
- and generally have a lack of self-esteem?
- Are you impatient?
- Are you jealous or envious?
- Do you hear voices, have nightmares
- and experience panic attacks?
- Are you a loner or feel out of touch?
- Are you blaming others for everything?
- Do you always have to be right?
- Do you feel bad about yourself?
- Do you have thoughts of suicide?
- Do you feel bad about yourself, ugly, fat, stupid...?

You know something has a strong hold on you when you start believing that this is who you are or who you have become. The stronghold becomes your identity. You decide that you are a loner. You decide you are shy or impatient. You label yourself as paranoid, anxious, an addict, a gambler, ADD.... We say things like, "I am just sensitive," when in fact we are touchy and easily offended. We say, "I am lazy, tired, sick, poor, perverted, or depressed."

These are strongholds, not character traits.
God did not make you this way.
You don't have to stay this way.

How does this happen? How do we lose control of our thoughts, feelings, moods, or our minds? And more importantly, how do we take back control?

Get ready for some good news.

You do not have to live with or accept every thought that comes into your mind. You are in control and master of your very own mind and thoughts. If a thought or thoughts start to bombard you, you can stop them. Your mind is yours, and it's off limits to outside forces of evil.

LET ME REPEAT this. Your mind is yours, and it's off limits to outside forces of evil.

You are in control and master of your very own mind and thoughts. You may not be able to deflect or control thoughts from coming yet, but in time you will. However, beginning today, you can control whether or not these thoughts take up residence.

It doesn't matter how long you have been behaving, thinking, or believing a certain way, you can change your mind and therefore, more importantly, change yourself. You can change your future and become someone you never thought you were capable of becoming. It starts now. CHOOSE today to grow into the spiritual powerhouse you were meant to be and believe God has the desire and means to get you there.

You can change your future and become the man or woman God meant for you to become. You can become the person no one else ever thought you were capable of becoming. You can do this through Christ. He is the answer. His power and love are running through your veins. He has a plan for your life, and it is better than anything you are currently experiencing. His plans are beyond your ability to even think of or imagine.

Jeremiah 29:11 *"For I know well the plans I have in mind for you — oracle of the Lord — plans for your welfare and not for woe, so as to give you a future of hope."*

We are the summation of all our thoughts. What kind of thoughts went into the development of your mind, your attitude, and your emotions? What made you the way you are? Why do we think the way we do and react the way we do? Why do we get moody or emotional? Why are we touchy and so easily offended? Why are we so needy and attracted to the wrong people? What is wrong with us?

Jesus came to this earth to break the power of Satan and to restore us to a right relationship with God the Father. Jesus came to fix us, heal us, restore us, and save us.

> **1 John 3:8** *"Indeed, the Son of God was revealed to destroy the works of the devil."*

Jesus has triumphed over the enemy, and because of Jesus, so have you. Jesus not only destroys the devil's stronghold over us but gives us power over the enemy as well. This is mind-boggling to me. Jesus gave us his name and the power and authority that come with it. You just don't know it yet. You have triumphed over the enemy. YOU!

> **Luke 10:19** *"Behold, I have given you the power 'to tread upon serpents' and scorpions and upon the full force of the enemy and nothing will harm you."*

Jesus is speaking to the 72 disciples He sent out two by two, not just the 12 apostles.

He gave them power to tread upon serpents and scorpions and upon the FULL force of the enemy. He did this for them and he has done it for you. You and I have been given power over depression, anxiety, addiction, fear, and sin. Still don't believe you have power over the enemy? Listen to what Jesus said to all of us believers.

> **Mark 16:17** *"These signs will accompany those who believe: in my name they will drive out demons..."*

Who is Jesus talking to? Those who believe, you and me. If you are a believer, this is God's plan for you. God has given you the power to use His name to drive out demons. WHO? You! How do I know this? Jesus said, "These signs will accompany those who believe." Jesus is talking about believers, not just Bishops, Cardinals, or priests. He is not talking about apostles, but everyday believers like you and me. Where does this power come from? How do we get it? Through Jesus. All through Him. He won it for us by dying on the cross and then passed His authority and power on to us through the Holy Spirit who lives in us.

> **2 Corinthians 5:17-18** *"So whoever is in Christ is a new creation: the old things have passed away; behold, new things have come. And all this is from God, who has reconciled us to himself through Christ."*

A stronghold will not yield to our power, but it must yield to the power of God in us. Is Jesus your power? Make Him your safe place, your refuge. For He is our rock, our fortress, and our deliverer from evil and all evil strongholds.

Psalm 18:1-3(4) *"I love you, Lord, my strength, Lord, my rock, my fortress, my deliverer, My God, my rock of refuge, my shield, my saving horn, my stronghold! Praised be the Lord, I exclaim! I have been delivered from my enemies."*

Have you surrendered to Jesus and given Him control?

When Jesus died on the cross, he defeated sin and every stronghold. He died to free you from sin and all the consequences of sin. Sin and death were defeated for every believer when Jesus died on the cross. Confess your sins, and Jesus is faithful to forgive your sins and all the effects of sin as well. God sent Jesus to deliver us from all the power of darkness. You may not know it yet. You may not be experiencing it yourself yet, but God freed you from every fear and worry, and situation you may find yourself in. Give God a chance to turn your life around. Give yourself to Him. Let Him take over.

Choose today to be made new in Christ Jesus. Declare your allegiance out loud. WORDS are powerful and effective. God created the universe with a word. Jesus healed the centurion's servant with just a word. Jesus is the Word. Words are powerful and so are yours. God made them that way. Your words do a ton of damage to the kingdom of Satan when you profess Jesus as your Lord. The devil hates hearing that name and for this reason, goes to great lengths to get us to misuse it.

Romans 10:9–13 *"For, if you confess with your mouth that Jesus is Lord and believe in your heart that God raised him from the dead, you will be saved. For one believes with the heart and so is justified, and one confesses with the mouth and so is saved. For the scripture says, 'No one who believes in him will be put to* *shame.' For there is no distinction between Jew and Greek; the same Lord is Lord of all, enriching all who call upon him. For "everyone who calls on the name of the Lord will be saved."*

At the back of this book is a prayer of surrender and commitment. What have you got to lose? You have everything to gain.

As you read this, believe that you are going to rise up and be the man or woman God has created you to be. You are putting yourselves in His hands. You are no longer at the mercy of the wind and the waves. You are not at the mercy of every circumstance any longer. You are in control. You are not just blowing in the wind. You have been transferred out of the darkness and into the light of the Son.

Believe that your life is about to change for the better.

3

NEGATIVE THOUGHTS

Negative thoughts are real and can consume you, overwhelm you, and control you. Negative thoughts come, but they don't have to stay. Thoughts come, but they do not have to be entertained, invited, or tolerated in any way or for any length of time. We do not have to take ownership of a thought just because it enters our mind. Many thoughts are lies. You don't have to believe them or obey them or even listen to them. Not all thoughts are yours; not all thoughts come from you. This may surprise you, but many thoughts come from evil spiritual forces.

Evil spiritual forces? Does this sound spooky or ridiculous to you? Negative thoughts are demonic. Listen and see for yourself. Jesus said, "The enemy comes to kill, steal, and destroy" (John 10:10). The same can be said for negative thoughts; they too kill, steal, and destroy.

Does the devil really exist? Do we have an enemy in heavenly places? (Demons are said to occupy heavenly places; not "Heaven" as we know it, but they are in a spiritual realm.)

Here are some scriptural references regarding demonic forces at work against us.

1 John 5:19 *"We know that we are children of God and that the world around us is under the control of the evil one."*

John 10:10 *"The thief comes only to kill, steal, and destroy. I have come that they may have life and have it to the full."*

1 Peter 5:8–9 *"Stay alert! Watch out for your great enemy, the devil. He prowls around like a roaring lion, looking for someone to devour."*

Ephesians 6:11–12 *"Put on the armor of God so that you may be able to stand firm against the tactics of the devil. For our struggle is not with flesh and blood but with the principalities, with the powers, with the world rulers of this present darkness, with the evil spirits in the heavens."*

James 4:7 *"Submit yourselves, then, to God. Resist the devil and he will flee from you."*

John 8:44-45 *(Jesus is speaking)"You belong to your father the devil and you willingly carry out your father's desires. He was a murderer from the beginning and does not stand in truth, because there is no truth in him. When he tells a lie, he speaks in character, because he is a liar and the father of lies. But because I speak the truth, you do not believe me."*

We have been raised in this world, but Jesus wants us in His world. He wants us in His Kingdom so He came to earth and rescued us Himself.

Col 1:13 *"For He has rescued us from the dominion of darkness and brought us into the kingdom of the Son He loves."*

If we have been rescued from the dominion of darkness, then the evil one has no power over us. Jesus rescued us, and He did a good job of it. Consider yourself rescued. Consider yourself saved. Consider yourself transferred into the Kingdom of Jesus.

The devil wants you to think you are still under his control, but you are not. When you feel down or tormented or worthless or a failure regarding spiritual or worldly matters, remember that these feelings do not originate from God. The devil wants to determine how you think, how you feel, and how you behave. So he places thoughts in your mind.

You have to remember that they are just thoughts, just feelings. We give them too much power.

We have been entertaining and believing these thoughts for so long we believe them to be who we are. We think, "I am a liar, a cheater, a sex fiend, a drunk, depressed, a worrier, unsociable, shy, mean, awkward, unfit, unattractive, an addict, a smoker, weak, sick..." But just because you think it or feel it, doesn't mean it's true; doesn't mean it is who you are.

Isn't it a relief to know those horrible thoughts that come into your mind are not yours, and you don't have to claim them as your own or keep them? I know right now you are thinking to yourself, "But these are my thoughts; this IS me, this is the way I think of myself." It may very well be the way you are, but are you ready for the NEW YOU? The "REAL" you. The YOU, you were meant to be, created to be.

You and I have a choice, the same choice Adam and Eve had to believe God and receive His gifts, or believe the enemy and receive His gifts, his thoughts, his ideas and plans for your life. The devil will always try to drag you down. He wants you down in the pit with him. As long as we are down in the pit or "in the gutter," the devil is happy and has us right where he wants us.

One day I was praying with someone who was in extreme fear and stress. Her chest was tight, and her head was pounding. The stress was causing her severe chest pains. I asked her if it was her heart, she assured me it was stress. We prayed together, and in the name of Jesus came against the spirit of anxiety and fear. I prayed with her until she rose up and walked. We prayed and stood our ground against the tactics of the devil until her chest stopped hurting and peace returned. The devil is relentless but completely defeated. Her thoughts had her convinced she was never going to be well and was only going to get worse. We believe the devil is powerful and we believe the symptoms are real and too powerful for us.

I prayed with a young man who was sure he had schizo-phrenia. He was terrorized into believing it was true. The devil will stop at nothing to keep us tormented and in fear. But thankfully he came for prayer. This is where the lies are exposed. Call someone who knows Jesus and isn't afraid to pray. If you are tormented by thoughts, stay tuned and get free.

Negative thoughts keep us ensnared, trapped and chained. But because we are "IN CHRIST" those chains are broken. There is no trap, no chain, and nothing has us bound.

One acronym for Fear is "False Evidence Appearing Real." Fear is FALSE. The devil uses fear to scare and threaten. He only succeeds when we believe his lies, his carefully planted thoughts. Sometimes we need help fighting; we can't fight him alone. We need others to come alongside us. Do not be afraid to call for help. The Bible says one can chase 1,000 foes but two can chase 10,000 (Leviticus 26:8). Your foe is not flesh and blood but evil rulers and authorities in the unseen world.

> **Ephesians 6:12** *"For we are not fighting against flesh-and blood enemies, but against evil rulers and authorities of the unseen world, against mighty powers in this dark world, and against evil spirits in the heavenly places."*

Why do I talk so much about the devil? Why? Because once he is exposed as nothing but a liar, you are set free because you know who and what you are up against; the liar and his lies. I want you free from the grasp of terror, nightmares, and negative thoughts. RECOGNIZING these thoughts as lies is half the battle. Once you recognize these thoughts as just thoughts planted to terrorize you, you can say, "OH, IT'S JUST YOU! HA! The Greater One lives in me!"

This story has been passed down over the centuries and is so worth telling. One day a saint woke up in the middle of the night and saw Satan himself standing at the foot of his bed. He woke with a start and said, "Oh, it's just you! Greater is He that is in me than he that is the world," and the saint rolled over and went back to sleep.

> **1 John 4:4** *"For the one who is in you is greater than the one who is in the world."*

Here are some examples of negative thoughts that we entertain, thoughts we file away, hold onto, and eventually believe about ourselves.

- I am a failure.
- I am useless.
- I am fat, ugly, and old.
- I am screwed up.
- I am perverted.
- I am a bad mother/father.
- I am a sinner who keeps on sinning.
- I'll never get it right.
- I am out of my mind.
- I will grow old all alone.
- No future for me.
- I am not going to make it.
- I won't have enough.
- I am going to get sick and die.
- I will get cancer.
- I have gone too far.
- I am going insane.
- They will lock me up.
- They hate me.
- No one likes me.
- No one needs me.
- No one will take care of me.
- He doesn't care about me.
- I am hopeless,
- No one appreciates me.
- God doesn't have time for me.
- God hates me.

Here are some other examples of negative thoughts or attitudes we practice. These words come out of our mouths so readily because they are lurking in our mind all the time. These thoughts occupy our mind and have become our default thoughts, and therefore they show up in our everyday language. They come out of us on a regular basis or when triggered by some outside influence.

- I hate my life.
- I hate my clothes.
- I hate my house.
- I hate my boss.
- I hate my job.
- I hate my hair, my teeth, my nose...
- I hate her.
- I hate him.
- I can't work.
- I can't move.
- I can't think.
- I can't feel.
- I can't love.
- I can't forgive.
- I can't live.
- I can't go.
- I can't do it.
- I just can't.
- You don't understand.
- How dare she?
- Who does he think he is?
- She has no right.
- How could he do this to me?
- I can't let her get away with it.
- It's not fair.
- Why do I have to put up with this?
- He can't do anything right.
- She will never amount to anything.
- He is lazy, good for nothing.
- She will get sick and die.

- He is an idiot.
- Should never have married him.
- He is nothing but a drunk.
- I deserve better.
- She makes me sick.
- He makes me crazy.
- What a jerk.
- It's all her fault.

We cannot allow these thoughts to reside in us, or we will become as ugly as they sound. They will literally make us sick. We need to undo/recall/delete/erase/unlearn them.

We were not made this way. We are not made to be fearful, anxious and depressed. We were made to live. When thoughts become a habit, we become enslaved to fear, anxiety and depression and a stronghold develops.

WORRY AND FEAR are devastating and debilitating. Worry is meditating on the devil's thoughts. Worry is full of doubt. I can't say it any plainer than this, worry is a lack of trust in the Lord. When you worry, you are trusting in your-self and not God. When you are trusting in your own strength, you have cause to worry. When you are worried or fearful you are really saying to God, "I believe you will forsake me. I believe you will fail me." That is what God hears every time you worry.

Read these scriptures below and believe they are meant for you.

> **Deuteronomy 20:4** *"For it is the Lord, your God, who goes with you to fight for you against your enemies and give you victory."*

Deuteronomy 3:22 *"Do not fear them, for it is the Lord, your God, who will fight for you."*

Deuteronomy 31:6 *"Be strong and steadfast; have no fear or dread of them, for it is the Lord, your God, who marches with you; he will never fail you or forsake you."*

When you are worried or fearful it may help to remember these are just thoughts trying to steal your peace. You don't have to be controlled by them.

You have authority over your mind and your thoughts. You get to choose what you meditate on.

This may be news to you, but we do not have to allow negative thoughts to invade the privacy of our brains. Our minds are OURS! Are you ready to take back what is yours and take control and ownership of your very own mind? YOU CAN and you will! Jesus said we could, and He has equipped us with the power and authority to do it. We don't have to allow a thought in any more than we would let a stranger, a pig, or a snake into our home.

Once I was on a plane from Dallas to Cleveland when I saw myself in a steel tube in the sky, and I started to freak out. I was having a panic attack. The plane was closing in on me and I wanted to get out. I began to panic. I had to get to the back of the plane. I pushed my way passed the stewards and made my way to the restroom. I started to hyperventilate and I had a vision of myself lying on the floor foaming at the mouth. I kept praying and saying, "Please, Lord, help me; I trust you." Nothing changed. I kept repeating, "I trust you, Jesus" as I waited for the lavatory. There was a mother and child next to me. I looked at the child and everything started to get fuzzy. Time was running out. I had to get into the restroom and fast. I started to break out in a cold sweat. I wondered what I looked like.

The door opened and I entered and, in front of the mirror, looking at myself, I heard the Holy Spirit say, "**It's just a thought.**" The words echoed in my mind: It's just a thought; yes, it's just a thought! I am not going to be taken down by a thought! NO WAY! I looked at myself and commanded my thoughts into obedience, saying, "Thoughts, I command you into obedience. I command you to obey Jesus. Jesus is my Lord and the Lord of my mind." Immediately I was fine and went back to my seat and sat down without a trace of fear or terror. I was back to normal and elated!

COMMAND those thoughts to leave! You can do it. You are allowed to do it. And you must. You have to know, that as a child of God, you have the authority to command these wicked thoughts to leave your mind. You have the authority over sickness and depression and moodiness, etc., because Jesus gave it to you. This authority is given to believers. Quit living a defeated life.

How do we rid ourselves of these thoughts? How do we do it?

> 1. *BELIEVE it's possible and that there is a bright future for you.*
> 2. *INVITE THE HOLY SPIRIT and His power and influence.*
> 3. *RECOGNIZE the negative thoughts and where they come from.*
> 4. *FIGHT. Persevere and DO IT!*

1. BELIEVE

Know that VICTORY IS SURE and it's yours. Believe it's possible to change your thoughts. The Bible tells us what and how to think in Philippians, Chapter 4. If God tells us what to think about, then it must be doable. There is a way to stop the evil thoughts and keep them from entering.

> **Phil 4:8** *"Fix your thoughts on what is true, and honorable, and right, and pure, and lovely, and admirable. Think about things that are excellent and worthy of praise."*

FIX YOUR THOUGHTS ON SOMETHING ELSE - Start thinking new thoughts. The mind can't think of two things at once. God tells us in His word what to think on.

DO IT IMMEDIATELY, so you don't get sucked in. Don't let a passing thought become a stronghold. Know and believe that God's will and desire are to heal you and lift you out and away from negative thoughts, depression, and the pit of despair.

Know who you are and what is yours, what is rightfully yours! You are not the old you anymore. You have been born again. Yes, you have. You wouldn't still be reading this if you weren't part of God's kingdom. Don't keep doubting it. Don't doubt the new you. You are not doomed to repeat your same mistakes and remain stuck and imprisoned. Jesus came to set the prisoners free. Free from our very own selves and our own mindsets.

There is only one way into God's kingdom and it's through Jesus. You want to be born again, BORN of the SPIRIT. Who wouldn't want freedom? Who wouldn't want a do-over? Jesus said you must be born again. Say goodbye to your old, unfulfilling life and yes to a new life in Christ. You are a new creation in Christ. You received an inheritance when you were born into God's family. You inherited the kingdom. It's time to find out what you received in the will when Jesus died for you. Yes, you inherited the throne.

You are unique and precious to God. You are His one and only. There is only one of you. And for you, He was willing to give up His son. God paid a high price for you. God did not spare His only son for you, so why would He withhold love, healing, forgiveness, joy, prosperity?

> With God all things are possible **(Matthew 19:26)**. Jesus said WHAT? "Everything is possible for the one who has faith" **(Mark 9:23)**.

2. HOLY SPIRIT

You need the Holy Spirit. You can't do it alone. Jesus said in Luke 24:49 "And [behold] I am sending the promise of my Father (the Holy Spirit) upon you; but stay in the city until you are clothed with power from on high." The Holy Spirit is not an option, which is why we, as Catholics, are confirmed. Confirmation is a sacrament where we receive the power of the Holy Spirit as adult Christians and choose the gifts of the Holy Spirit for ourselves.

Paul says to seek the gifts of the Holy Spirit earnestly (1 Cor 12:31). Jesus said to His disciples before ascending into heaven, "Wait, don't leave Jerusalem, but wait for the promise of the Father, the Holy Spirit. You will receive power when the Holy Spirit comes upon you, and you will be my witnesses."

Acts 1:4-5 and 8 *"While meeting with them, he enjoined them not to depart from Jerusalem, but to wait for "the promise of the Father about which you have heard me speak; 5 for John baptized with water, but in a few days you will be baptized with the holy Spirit.".... 8 But you will receive power when the holy Spirit comes upon you, and you will be my witnesses in Jerusalem, throughout Judea and Samaria, and to the ends of the earth."*

3. RECOGNIZE

Recognize the enemy. Recognize the good thoughts from the bad, the devil's thoughts from your own. As long as you remain in the dark, he can control you by letting you think it's just who you are. As soon as you recognize that these thoughts are from that slimy devil, victory is sure. You have won. It's almost that simple.

Recognition IS KEY. If you learn one thing from this book, learn this. NOT EVERY THOUGHT IS YOURS. The devil is tricky, sly, relentless, but utterly powerless over you. He cannot do anything to you if you belong to Christ. I learned long ago that I never have to fear him. He is nothing but dust under my feet. He just wants you to think he is big, scary, and powerful. Once you know a thought is evil and bent on destroying you, it's easy to reject this thought.

Recognize negative thoughts.

Negative thoughts are damaging thoughts, depressing thoughts, critical thoughts, suicidal thoughts, perverted thoughts, thoughts about others, nervous, fearful, anxious, and sinful thoughts. Thoughts that rehash hurts are negative thoughts. Every time you think about how someone hurt you, STOP, DROP, AND ROLL.

STOP! Make a purposeful decision to REJECT those THOUGHTS.

Say it. "Thoughts, I reject you. I may have invited you, accepted you, and agreed with you, but now I reject you. I renounce you. You are not welcome. I command my thoughts into obedience to Jesus Christ my Lord."

When you get a thought such as, "I hate..." know that this is not who you really are. This is not you. NIP IT IN THE BUD. Do not let it take root. You are not a hater. You do not hate. You may feel hatred, but it is not who you are. You are a new creation in Christ.

Don't accept what these thoughts are saying about "YOU." Do not accept them as yours or who you are. Drive the thought out no matter how tempting it is to continue entertaining this thought. It may be gratifying, but it is deadly. Your flesh will want to stay there, but this thought will corrupt you, kill you, and destroy you and your relationships.

Recognize it as a lie and renounce it. Reject the thought and refuse to allow it to stay. Begin by never allowing the words to form. Don't say "I hate _____," no matter how tempting. Know that you are a prince or princess of the Kingdom and these thoughts are unbefitting royalty. Be determined, purposeful, and mindful. You are Godly.

You are in control, not the thought. Remember, IT'S JUST A THOUGHT.

4. FINALLY - ACT - FIGHT

FIGHT. Be purposeful and tenacious. Be committed. Fear and worry will not give up without a fight. How determined are you? Will you cave at the first sign of a push back? Be tenacious, the fear that has held you for so long will not leave unless it knows and believes you are serious and mean what you say.

Recurring thoughts that have become strongholds and have gained a foothold are not willing to just pick up and leave just because you say so. Worry, anxiety, and doubt are not just going to run when they see you coming with a new conviction. They will test your resolve. Moodiness, sickness, jealousy, addictions, rage, and temper tantrums will not give up territory without a fight. Don't back down.

Sometimes we are delivered immediately and miraculously. Sometimes we have to fight with faith as God stretches us and teaches us. Don't just live with it. Many people believe this is just a cross they have to bear. This is just not true. These are not tools God uses.

Would You Let a Snake Stay in Your Living Room?

Just because you find a snake in the middle of your living room doesn't mean it has to stay there. Just because it got in doesn't mean it has to be fed and entertained. We don't wine and dine unwanted guests. If you came home and found a snake in the middle of your living room, would you tell your family that they just have to deal with it? Would you say, "You're just going to have to get used to it — live with it?" Would you tell your children to try to stay out of its way? NO! You would chop off its head! We don't live with snakes, so why live with strongholds (depression, anger, fear, insecurity, hatred, etc.)? They want us, they want to control us, but they can't have us. You have to get to the point where you will no longer tolerate these strongholds.

I read a book once called *Pigs in the Parlor*. It was about the devil and his demons taunting us, describing their activity against Christians in this way. Imagine you have pigs in your parlor or dining room. What are you going to do? Are you going to ask them to leave, beg them to leave, cry, and complain? Or, do you entertain them and keep cleaning up after them? Do you tolerate or ignore them, hoping they will just go away, or are you going to drive them out?

> **2 Corinthians 10:3-5** *"For though we live in the world, we do not wage war as the world does. The weapons we fight with are not the weapons of the world. On the contrary, they have divine power to demolish strongholds. We demolish arguments and every pretension that sets itself up against the knowledge of God, and we take captive every thought to make it obedient to Christ."*

COMMAND your thoughts into obedience like the Bible tells you to. You are in charge. It is your mind, after all. TRY IT. Don't be shy. Say this out loud, "Memories, thoughts, leave me! There is a new sheriff in town; His name is Jesus. Jesus is Lord of my mind. I command you to go in the name of my Lord Jesus." Jesus left us His name. Don't be afraid to use it.

Okay, let's get real. SAY THIS....

> *"Suicidal thoughts, leave me. I command you to leave me in the name of Jesus. Jesus is Lord of my mind."*

Remember, they are just thoughts trying to consume you and drive you.

> *"Critical thoughts, leave me....."* *"Hateful thoughts leave me...."*
> *"Perverted thoughts, leave me......."* *"I am who God says I am,*
> *not what thoughts say I am."*

God never leads us into the pit; we do that ourselves. He neither leads us to the pit nor leaves us there. No matter how we got there or how lo ng we have been there, His plan is always to lift us up and out. So don't believe the negative thoughts. Stop believing it's just your lot in life; you got yourself into this; you're stuck here; you deserve this; you are a cheater, liar, hopeless. God lifts us up and never brings us down. It doesn't matter how many times you fail; He is always there to pick you up and set you on the right course.

You wouldn't still be reading this if you were a quitter. You are coming out of the pit step by step unless you give up and quit. It's never too late for redemption, conversion, or forgiveness. God always has time for you. You are never too much trouble for Him; He is still there for you.

Sometimes we think God has better things to do than worry about us. This is just not true. God doesn't have anything better to do than take care of you. You are that important to Him. Remember the two thieves crucified on the cross next to Jesus; only one was in his right mind and turned to Jesus. He knew it was not too late. Make Jesus' day and turn to Him and begin the journey upward.

THAT IS ALL THE MAN ON THE CROSS NEXT TO JESUS HAD TO DO. TURN TO JESUS. Jesus didn't say, "Go to confession first, go through RCIA (Rite of Christian Initiation of Adults), go to church." The man didn't even confess his sins. He acknowledged his faith in Jesus Christ. You can do it now. Turn to Him. Jesus will lead you to church, confession, RCIA. Don't worry about that, first get yourself to Jesus. Jesus always leads us to His Church.

There is only one way into the Kingdom of God and it's through faith, faith in Jesus Christ. He is waiting. He wants you now just the way you are. Don't clean up first. Let Him do that.

Father, I pray for the man or woman reading this right now. Speak to them, minister Your love and mercy to them. May they feel Your presence and hunger and thirst for You. You promise us that we will find You when we seek You diligently. Help us to seek You and to be diligent about it.

> *May I take this opportunity to tell you something? There is no lesson to be learned in the pit except the way out, and the way out is Jesus. Hang on for dear life, and you will come out!"*

Jesus lives. Jesus wins. We belong to Him. The devil will fill our minds with thoughts that tell us the opposite, that we don't deserve Him. But the truth is we belong to Him.

Rom 8:31 *"If God is for us who can be against us?"*

Without Jesus, we are at the mercy of principalities, and spiritual forces of evil. With Jesus, we are more than conquerors. We can overcome anything, even Satan himself.

God has given us the tools. He wants us armed and dangerous. You need this for yourself, your family, the generations to come, and the world around you. You will learn what to say, how to say it, why to say it, and what SPEAKING ALOUD DOES for you and to the enemy. YOU are going to make a difference in this world.

The buck stops with you.

You are not letting this continue. You are making a stand. You are taking a stand against these strongholds and negative thoughts and attitudes and doing it for your sake and the sake of those coming after you. It may have come to you through your bloodline, but it stops here. Continue reading about depression and generational curses/strongholds and get ready for the cure.

4

DEPRESSION

Thoughts are like trains, they take you somewhere. One thought leads to another, and if your thoughts are negative, you will soon end up in a place called "FUNKVILLE." The more you follow a thought to Funkville, the easier it is to get there. Your mind just starts taking you there automatically. You begin to lose control. One little thought or memory can trigger the downward spiral, and soon you are full speed ahead to Funkville. If you do end up in Funkville, don't stay there. There is a way out.

You were not made to handle Funkville, so don't stay. It may have become a comfortable place for you. You may have been there so long you don't know how to leave, or you may have lost directions home. FUNKVILLE is not God's design or desire for you; it is not God's destination for you ever. God has the ticket out, and it is yours for free.

Depression comes from many different sources, but no matter where it comes from or how it got to you, it is time for depression to hit the road. I believe depression is the devil's favorite tool against the body of Christ. No matter how long you have lived with it or how "clinical" or "medical" it is, it is time for it to go. It is not God's will or plan for your life. Believe that! Depression, in any and all of its forms (whether diagnosed or not), is a tormenting spirit and is not yours to keep.

You may have a severe case, and it may be quite dangerous, but know that its hold over you has been conquered and demolished. The chains have been loosened, and the straps that have bound you have been severed. You have been set free, and it is time to receive that freedom and walk in it. This freedom comes with faith and trust in the One that set you free. It is happening one day at a time, or all at once, but it IS happening. It may not feel like it is happening but it is. Have Faith. Faith is not seeing or feeling but believing. Trust the one who is trustworthy.

> **Luke 1:68** *"Praise be to the Lord, the God of Israel, because he has come to his people and redeemed them."*

You have been redeemed and purchased for freedom. Thefreedictionary.com says this about the word redeemed: "to buy or pay off; clear by payment; to recover ownership of by paying a specified sum." The word redeemed was used in the slave market, basically you were released from slavery by payment of a sum. Jesus ransomed us. He is our redeemer.

Jesus paid with His blood for our lives. So start living. You were once a slave to sin and the worries and cares of this world, but you have been redeemed. You have been purchased and transferred to a new kingdom, God's kingdom here on earth. You have a new Lord and master now, Jesus. You were a slave to fear and evil and now you are a slave to righteousness. The devil will keep us in chains forever if we let him.

I Corinthians 7:23 *"You were bought at a price;"*

I Corinthians 6:19-20 *"You are not your own; you were bought at a price."*

What does it mean "you were bought?" When Satan entered the Garden of Eden in Genesis Chapter 3, he stole the keys to dominion over the earth from Adam and Eve. They died that day. They became spiritually dead and because of them so did we. Adam and Eve sold themselves into slavery to the Devil. Jesus called the devil the "ruler of this world" (see John 14:30). God gave DOMINION to Adam and Eve and they turned around and gave their authority and power to SATAN in the Garden.

They became slaves and "sinners." This is why we are all born with original sin. We all became sinners. That was our inheritance through Adam and Eve. We inherited a sinful nature. You don't have to teach us to sin, it comes naturally. We are sinners by nature. Jesus came to give us a new nature and a new heritage. We are now heirs of God's Kingdom. Jesus came to rescue Adam and Eve and all of their children and restore them to life. That is, you and me. He rescued us from darkness, sin, and all the works of evil. We have been transferred, the Bible says, from the Kingdom of darkness to the Kingdom of the Son.

Colossians 1:13-14 *"He delivered us from the power of darkness and transferred us to the kingdom of his beloved Son, in whom we have redemption, the forgiveness of sins."*

We will remain slaves, however, if we don't know we have been set free. We will remain accused if we don't know we are forgiven. The devil loves to lie to us and it brings him great joy when we believe his lies. So don't remain accused just because the accuser is reminding you of every sin you ever committed. We will remain condemned and shamed if we don't believe Jesus' death took care of EVERY sin, past, present, and future. We will remain sick if we don't believe he healed us. If we believe we are under a curse instead of "ransomed from the curse," it will continue to have power over us. Jesus paid the ransom to deliver us from every curse.

> **Galatians 3:13** *"Christ ransomed us from the curse of the law by becoming a curse for us"*

THIS IS HUGE, and we don't know about it. God paid a hefty price to set you free from every curse listed in the Bible. The price was the BLOOD OF JESUS. His death bought you life and freed you from sin and all the consequences that come from your sin.

PRAISE GOD!

You don't have to live with depression. It's not your burden to carry. Now believe it! BELIEVE more in the power of Jesus than in the power of depression to control you and ruin your life.

You may say, "Well, I don't feel free." Today is the first day of walking free. Freedom is not a feeling; it is a state of being, a right, and a privilege of the children of God. You are so used to feeling depressed and being depressed, and you have been lied to for so long, that it is hard to believe the truth.

Receive the truth today. Think of today as your first day of rehab. You are "rehabbing" the way you **THINK** and the way you **TALK** and eventually the way you **BELIEVE**.

It begins with the Word of God and surrendering to Jesus. If you have never done this for yourself, do it now. Say out loud, "Jesus, I choose You as my Lord and Savior. I believe You died for me and purchased for me a free ticket to heaven. I accept the invitation and thank You for it. I believe You not only died, but rose from the dead to bring me new life"

Think of depression as a tool from hell sent to attack you and harm you. God says that "EVERY weapon fashioned against you shall fail" (Isaiah 54:17). Depression has no right to you, no authority over you, and it has to go. It's time for you to rise up with power and destroy its hold on you, and you can do it beginning today because the Bible says that the Greater One lives in you.

> 1 **John 4:4** *"You belong to God, children, and you have conquered them, for the One who is in you is greater than the one who is in the world."*

In Him and connected to Him, you can do all things. Nothing is too difficult for you because you are in Him and He is in You. Who? Jesus. Jesus is more powerful than anything coming against you and now is your time to reclaim your life.

So, what are you waiting for? Do you really think God wants you depressed? Do you believe God is using this to teach you a lesson?

One definition of depression is "determination to reach a goal that is impossible to achieve." I was telling this to my neighbor. I told her, "One definition for depression is the determination or compulsion to reach a goal that is impossible to achieve." She said, "Oh, you mean like, I can never be a grandma because my only daughter just had a complete hysterectomy?" Yes, that would be a good example of an impossible goal.

Depression is to be routed and overthrown and today is the day. Not tomorrow, but today. It is time to be rescued by your knight in shining armor — JESUS. It's time to lift up your arms to the rescuer and trust Him to come for you. You may not "FEEL" it right away, but we don't walk by feeling, we walk by faith. Give yourself time to grow in faith. It will happen. You just have to keep your faith in Jesus.

Today is the day. If you are serious and have decided to trust Jesus and walk out of this PIT, then write this day down. Remember this day and remind yourself of your decision. Jesus already made the decision to save you and rescue you; it's up to you to come into agreement with Him and remain in agreement. The devil will push back; he will fight. Are you ready to STAND FIRM? Are you prepared to hold your ground? Don't let the symptoms keep you bound. Don't let the fact that you still feel depressed rob you of your confidence. HEALING IS SURE. Be willing to fight and don't give up.

Psalm 27:14 "*WAIT for the Lord, wait expectantly, for He shall surely come.*"

The world may say you are stuck with it, and you are in too deep, but God says that those who hope in HIM will renew their strength.

> **Isaiah 40:31** *"They will soar on wings like eagles, they will run and not grow weary, they will walk and not grow faint."*

> **Psalm 18:8** *"They confronted me in the day of my disaster, but the Lord was my support."*

This is for you, not just your neighbor or the holy woman who sits next to you in the pew — it is for YOU. It may not come tomorrow, but it will happen. Don't give up and don't quit believing. Strongholds like depression are not easily destroyed, but praise God that we are more than conquerors through Christ Jesus. If you are in Christ, if Christ lives in you (and He does or you wouldn't be reading this book), then you are a conqueror. You have a conquering spirit in you. Depression is not tolerated; it is conquered. The Bible says that EVERYTHING is possible for those who believe. Are you a believer? Do you want to go boldly where you have never gone before? You can and you will.

Jesus didn't rescue us just to see us miserable and in a pit. He didn't set us free to see us in bondage. We are no longer at the mercy of our past, our thoughts, our memories, or our dreams or nightmares. We are no longer at the mercy of our attitudes. We are over-comers.

But you say, "If this is true, then why does my past still haunt me? Why am I still depressed and hearing voices?" You and I live 24 hours a day, seven days a week in this world and give God only one or two hours a week. It's not enough. I didn't say you may get delivered; I said you would. Just be patient and hang on to Jesus. It's not a matter of will you, but when? Jesus came to deliver us, and it worked. It already happened. The devil will keep you from your victory your whole life if he can keep you distracted and in his grip. You can believe whoever you want to. Who do you want to believe? The liar is loud and speaking often on the television, in the news, and in the workplace. You have to separate yourself from this world so you can hear God.

> **Proverbs 4:20** *"My son, to my words be attentive, to my sayings incline your ear."*

Who are you listening to? To whom are you inclining an ear? Today is a new day. As part of your rehab, I want you to begin speaking to yourself. You have to speak! This is more important than you know. You have to see yourself as someone brand new and free and identify with this person. "YOU!" You have a new identity. Quit saying "I am so depressed, I hate my life, I want to die, I am bipolar." You become what you say about yourself. Change your words. It's time to identify with the new you; the new you were created to be. Start by speaking.

> *"I am a child of God. I am healed. I am content and cheerful and full of life. I love life and love my family. I am blessed and hopeful and Jesus is the joy of my life. I am healed."*
>
> Say, *"(your name)! rise today and walk."*

Today is the first day of the rest of your life. If you are depressed, sick, tired, or defeated, tell yourself this:

"I belong to Jesus. I am His son/daughter and depression/anxiety, you are trespassing on private property. Today is a great day. Jesus is Lord of my life. The Blood of Jesus has rescued me from the power of darkness. I am well. I am whole because Jesus made me whole. The Lord forgives all my sins and heals all my diseases. Jesus has redeemed me from the pit, and He crowns me with love and compassion. I am healed because He told us in Matthew Chapter Eight that He took my sickness and disease. He bore my sins and all my diseases on the cross. I get to say this, 'By His stripes, I am healed' because His word says so. My God has delivered me from the power of darkness and brought me into the kingdom of His Son. I am filled to overflowing with the Holy Spirit. The Holy Spirit lives in me. The Bible says, 'Greater is He that is in me than he that is in the world.' I command my mind to obey JESUS CHRIST. I take authority over my mind and command it to obey you Lord Jesus. You are LORD of my thoughts and my mind. I have the Mind of Christ" (Psalm 103:3, Isaiah 53, 1 John 4:4, 2 Cor 10:5, 1 Cor 2:16)

FOLLOW REHAB

You are stronger than you think you are because the Greater One lives inside of you. He does. He hasn't left you. Jesus is your Lord and your Savior. There is nothing you can do or say to drive Him away. He loves you and lives in you. You are still His prize, His child.

I am not saying you can do this alone, or that you should. Call someone. Call someone who will help you and pray with you. I have people calling me all the time for prayer! Call me. I am on the phone every day Monday thru Friday, starting at 7:00 a.m. Central Standard Time.

For more information and the phone number, send email to marybeth@spiritfilledcatholic.com

Sometimes we can't find someone when we need someone. Jesus is always there. One night my mother was sick and frightened. She called me in the middle of the night and I wasn't answering my phone, and neither was my husband. She had to go straight to God. She told me the next morning, "I am glad you didn't answer the phone. It forced me to trust God."

Jesus is greater than anything coming against you; depression, accusations, finances, memories, sin, and addiction. May your faith in Jesus way outshine your faith in depression's power over you. Don't give up waiting in faith, trust Jesus has this. The devil is not going to give you up without a fight, so why should you? Fight. Don't submit to him. Fight by speaking every day and read God's word aloud every day.

The devil will convince you he still has you, but he doesn't. EVERYTHING he does or says is a lie. Remind yourself every day who you are in Christ.

I am not a doctor, and I know many of us are diagnosed "clinically depressed" and under a doctor's care. I am not suggesting you leave the doctor or disregard him/her, but add this to your daily regimen. Add this prescription. There is a prescription you have been missing, and it just may be the answer.

PRESCRIPTION ...

   1. TAKE YOUR EYES OFF OF YOU. Start praying for others in the same situation as you. If you don't know anyone, ask the Holy Spirit to show you who

to pray for. Pray for those in the news, family members, people you met yesterday or will meet today. Do something for someone else.

2. PUT YOUR EYES ON GOD. He is the way out. Start praising Him. If you don't know how to praise Him, see below. Most of us don't know how to praise God. We are good at complaining and criticizing, but praise does not come naturally. Once you begin to glorify God something spiritual happens. God becomes magnified, and your problems pale in comparison. God wants an intimate daily relationship with you. Invite Him to be Lord and ruler. Pray and read His word daily.

3. SPEAK. Say, "Marybeth (your name)! rise up today and walk..." (See the previous page)

4. START WALKING - start going and doing what you couldn't or wouldn't do before. Do it trusting God will be with you and will protect you and come through for you.

5. JOIN A PRAYER GROUP OR BIBLE STUDY. You and I need accountability. We also need to be part of the body of Christ and minister to others and be ministered to.

Don't let those feelings fool you. Don't let those thoughts confuse you. **Those thoughts are talking to you, so you have to shut them up.** Change your atmosphere. It won't change itself. Do something. Go to your knees, change your position, run to God's word and start speaking to yourself. In the next chapter, you will learn how to change your mind and your thoughts.

5

CHANGE YOUR MIND – YOU CAN

Every time a thought or a memory comes to mind, we have a choice to reinforce it or dismiss it. When a negative, hurtful, or otherwise evil thought or memory is not driven out or nipped in the bud, we start believing it and agreeing with it. We can entertain them or cast them out. We can make room for them or kick them out. We can invite them to spend the night or drive them away. If we dwell on negative thoughts and allow them to set up camp in our minds, they will take up residence and become a stronghold that is not easily broken, healed, or overcome.

Someone once said, you may not be able to prevent a bird from flying over your head, but you can prevent that bird from making a nest in your hair. Just because a thought comes doesn't mean it has to stay.

Our brains know how to store thoughts and save them, filing them and even prioritizing them based on the amount of time we spend thinking about them. It is chemistry. I have no idea how it works, only that it's chemical and real. We don't have to follow our thoughts. Our minds can be changed, redirected, and refocused. We can change what we think about. The definition of mind according to Webster is "the element or complex of elements in an individual that feels, perceives, thinks, wills, and especially reasons." Our minds are our conscious and unconscious mental activity. I want my mind, my emotions, my perceptions, and automatic responses to be ruled and developed by my God and me, not by a whim, a trigger, a picture, memory, or my over active imagination.

We can change the way we think and what we think about. If God tells us what to think about, as He does in Philippians, then it must be doable.

> **Philippians 4:8** *"Finally, brethren, whatever things are true, whatever things are noble, whatever things are just, whatever things are pure, whatever things are lovely, whatever things are of good report, if there is any virtue and if there is anything praiseworthy — meditate on these things."*

If we are called by God to set our minds on things above, then it must be possible.

> **Colossians 3:1-2**"*Since, then, you have been raised with Christ, set your hearts on things above, where Christ is, seated at the right hand of God. Set your minds on things above, not on earthly things." (NIV - Biblegateway)*

We cannot think about two things at the same time, so if you don't like where your thoughts are going, change your mind by choosing to think of something else. Ask the Holy Spirit for help.

Ask Him to show you when you are going down that path that leads to "Funkville." Ask the Holy Spirit to warn you, to give you an opportunity to see and to recognize when you are about to spiral or lash out. Your mind right now has a default that needs to be reset. You have been reacting the same way for so long that it takes an effort to reset it. But it will obey. Don't give up. Jesus heals, and your mind will heal.

The Holy Spirit wants to walk with you and have a relationship with you. He is there for you. He doesn't have better things to do than help you. You are His desire.

"It doesn't matter how long you have been behaving, thinking, or believing a certain way, you can change your mind and therefore, more importantly, change you."

Remember, it's just a thought.

Thoughts are just that — thoughts. They can drive us, worry us, terrorize us, and control us. They are what the Bible calls "flaming arrows of the evil one" (**Ephesians 6:16**). The devil plants thoughts in our minds to keep us down and out. He is merciless, and when he finds which thoughts work, he won't let up. However, once we realize they are just thoughts, we can dismiss them or command them into obedience.

We have to be vigilant, diligent, and relentless. It's our mind, after all. Take authority and command your mind and your thoughts to obey.

One morning on our way to church, specific thoughts entered my mind and began to overwhelm me. Words began to well up inside of me. If they didn't come out, I was going to burst, so it was lecture time. I was convinced my teenagers needed to know how disappointed I was with them. They needed a lecture and they needed it now. I WAS SURE OF IT. I knew I was right.

The thoughts started to come, "How dare they get up late, they look like slobs, they need to clean their rooms and do their homework..." They needed to know it now on our way to church. If I didn't tell them what to expect when we got home, all hope would be lost.

The usual crazy impulse came and right before I began the lecture that would ruin the morning for all of us, I recognized that the thoughts didn't need to move me to action. I realized for the first time that I could decide to not go there. I chose to dismiss the thought and the whole lecture. I am the boss of me, the boss of my mind. I don't have to do what my mind tells me. I am in control of my mind.

Finally, I was listening to the Lord instead of the usual tirade of thoughts. He gave me a second to see the futility of my thoughts. The Holy Spirit gave me a chance to make it right. My eyes were opened before I let loose. It became so clear to me that I was about to ruin a perfectly wonderful morning. I decided at that moment that I would not let that thought rule. I just turned it off and trusted God.

It was so lovely to see it happen, to see it become a reality. *Thank you, Holy Spirit, for showing me and giving me that chance to choose.* Ask the Holy Spirit to give you an opportunity to choose correctly. Thoughts and reactions to thoughts can become very automatic after having lived that way for a long time.

Practice it. Be purposeful in your thinking.

I used to fly off the handle with my kids. I was following the Lord and had surrendered my life to Him, but still would fail more often than win. I was rude to my husband and mean to my mother. I couldn't seem to stop myself. Before I knew it, the words were out, and the damage was done, and I felt like a failure. I had no time to make a good decision because I was on autopilot and out of control.

A friend told me once to ask the Holy Spirit to "put a check in my spirit." Even a few seconds is enough to stop the response that comes automatically. Ask the Holy Spirit to give you a chance to respond correctly. Ask the Holy Spirit to give you a chance to do the right thing before the automatic response.

He did this for me. He truly is our helper. He wants you to succeed and is here to help you do just that. Call on Him. It may not happen overnight, but it will happen. God will not keep you the way you are.

> **John 14:26** *"The Advocate, the Holy Spirit that the Father will send in my name — He will teach you everything and remind you of all that I told you."*
>
> **Psalm 46:1** *"God is our refuge and strength, always ready to help in times of trouble."*

Ask the Holy Spirit to reveal to you the traps the devil has set up for you, those triggers that set you off. You have been on automatic for a long time, but now that is over. You are a new creature and God has transferred you out of darkness and into the kingdom of the Son He loves.

He will transform you into the real you. The YOU, you were created to be.

Are you easily offended? IT'S JUST A THOUGHT
Are you afraid? IT'S JUST A THOUGHT
Are you depressed? IT'S JUST A THOUGHT
Do you hate? IT'S JUST A THOUGHT
Memory or past hurts? IT'S JUST A THOUGHT
Unforgiveness? IT'S JUST A THOUGHT
Memory of a past Sin? IT'S JUST A THOUGHT

> **Romans 12:2** *"Do not conform yourselves to this age but be transformed by the renewal of your mind, that you may discern what is the will of God, what is good and pleasing and perfect."*

> **Colossians 1:13** *"He delivered us from the power of darkness and transferred us to the kingdom of his beloved Son."*

> **Isaiah 49:15–16** *"Can a mother forget her infant, be without tenderness for the child of her womb? Even should she forget, I will never forget you. See, upon the palms of my hands I have engraved you; your walls are ever before me."*

You are in control of your thoughts, so take control. TURN THE THOUGHT OFF. SAY NO. Make your mind obey you. Command your thoughts into obedience to Jesus.

HOW do you get rid of a thought? Start thinking of something else. Start singing a song. Start reading scripture out loud. Memorize Scripture so it's on your tongue and ready when you need it. Visualize something else. Picture something in your mind. Dr. John Hollar, former director of "Christ for the Nations" in Dallas, Texas, taught his students how to change their minds. He gave them this example. Picture in your mind the color red. Can you see it? Now stop visualizing red. It is hard to do. The students were still seeing red until he said, "Now picture yellow." Once your mind has something else to focus on, it's easy to change your mind.

Start praising God. Start declaring the opposite. We can't think about two things at once. You can't be fearful and faithful at the same time. You will be one or the other. The choice is yours. If you find yourself fearful, recognize that faith has slipped away. Change your mind. Faith is a gift of the Holy Spirit. Faith has been given to us. We have all received a measure of faith (Romans 12:3). Don't let fear displace it. Turn back to faith. Say to yourself,

"I choose to believe."

Words have the Power to Change our Thoughts

Words have power. We know that God's words are powerful, He made heaven and earth with His words. We know Jesus' words are powerful. Jesus used His words to command the wind and the waves. Even sickness and disease obeys His word.

Jesus gave us the same power! He gave us the power to speak to mountains. (See chapter "TOOLS FOR BATTLE - YOUR MOUTH")

Our words are powerful. We can make or break someone's day with just a word. We can make or break our own day with just a word. We can speak life or death to every situation. Every negative word we say or think brings us down. Speak life and receive the benefits of life. When you speak words that build someone up, you benefit as well. The Bible says you eat the fruit of your words.

Proverbs 18:21 *"Death and life are in the power of the tongue; those who choose one shall eat its fruit.*

Are you eating the wrong fruit? What words are nourishing you? Are you negative because that is what you hear all day coming out of your mouth? We can't control what comes out of other people's mouths. Sometimes we have to put up with negativity in our environment, but we CAN control ourselves. What you hear coming out of your own mouth will change your mind, your mood, your attitude, in time your circumstances, and eventually your entire life. You can't speak negatively and expect positive results. You can't put yourself or someone else down and expect to rise up. Change your mind and your thoughts by changing your words. Let me show you what I mean.

What comes to us through our ears influences what we think about. What we think about comes out of your mouth and what comes out of our mouth goes back into our ears which reinforces or influences our thinking. It becomes a cycle. We feed on negativity over and over again. Something has to break the cycle. How do we change our thoughts and our words and ultimately our feelings and attitudes.

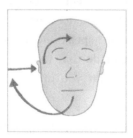

CHANGE YOUR WORDS. It will break the cycle. Let me give you an example.

Thought: "I hate him." You remember something and it triggers thoughts and you let that sentence come out of your mouth, "I hate him." We have a tendency to let everything come out of our mouth. We say things like; "He is lazy, rude, inconsiderate, thoughtless. I am sick of him. How dare he? He will never change." These words come out and reinforce our thoughts and we are trapped.

It takes being purposeful to change your thoughts. Force yourself to say the opposite. It may not feel right, but do it for God's sake if not his sake. It is possible to change your thoughts. It may take work because your flesh doesn't want to change.

Say, "I love him. He is a good man. Jesus loves him and died for him and has great plans for him. He is fearfully and wonderfully made." Don't wait until your thoughts are triggered to speak. Say it when things are cool and get your mind used to hearing it. Something supernatural happens when we start speaking. TRY IT.

START reading the word of God out-loud. Faith comes from hearing the word of God, the Bible says. Your faith will grow as you read God's Word. Again, it's supernatural. Your mind will change. You can influence your mind by what you say and re-train it. You can't speak one thing and think another. Our minds weren't made that way. If you want to change your mind change what you are saying. Your mind will follow your words.

We like to complain. Complaining comes to us naturally, but if we persist in complaining we will reap the dead fruit complaining brings. Be careful and watch what comes out of your mouth. Be vigilant.

On the night before the Israelites were to enter and take the land that God had promised them, they complained to God.

They were afraid of the so called "giants" living in the land. The Israelites, after Moses was sent to free them from slavery in Egypt, left and were journeying though the desert on their way to the "promised land." Just as they reached the land, they freaked out. They began to fear the inhabitants of the land and refused to obey God.

They refused to trust God and preferred slavery rather than receive the land that God promised them. God was so furious with His people that he led them through the desert until everyone who complained died. The people complained and said, "We are going to die, we will never make it, our bodies are going to fall here in the desert." God gave them the fruit of their words. They received exactly what they **SAID**.

> **Numbers 14-26-30** *"The Lord also said to Moses and Aaron:* ^{27} *How long will this wicked community grumble against me? I have heard the grumblings of the Israelites against me.* ^{28} *Tell them: "By my life I will do to you just what I have heard you say.* ^{29} *Here in the wilderness your dead bodies shall fall. Of all your men of twenty years or more, enrolled in your registration, who grumbled against me,* ^{30} *not one of you shall enter the land where I solemnly swore to settle you, except Caleb, son of Jephunneh, and Joshua, son of Nun."*

If you keep complaining about how sick and tired you are, you just may remain sick and tired. We get what we say. Change what you are saying. Make sure you aren't complaining. Every time I catch myself complaining I change my words. The words, "I am so sick" would love to come out of my mouth and just when they are about to, I recognize them and change my tune.

I immediately change my words to *"I am well in the name of Jesus. Thank you for my health Lord, sickness is far from me. You carried my diseases and bore my sickness, I am well. I am healthy because you healed me. I choose to receive the healing you paid a dear price to give me."*

God was so angry with the Israelites for their lack of trust and grumbling that he punished them by forcing them to remain in the wilderness (in the desert) for 40 years. 40 years! God waited till every single person who complained died.

It took 40 years for what should have been an 11 day journey. Why was God so angry and His punishment so severe? The people had just witnessed the Red Sea open up before their eyes. They had witnessed the Nile River turn to blood. They were just spared their first born child while every first born Egyptian male perished before their eyes. They had seen God move mightily for them and still they would not believe Him or trust Him or follow Him.

Ask the Holy Spirit for Help

Jesus said regarding the Holy Spirit, He will teach you everything. Remind yourself who you are, to whom you belong, and the power you have over the enemy. The choice is yours because you are in control, you just don't know it or believe it yet.

One of the enemy's greatest tools is condemnation. He plays this card whenever we are vulnerable. If he can get us to believe we are undeserving or unworthy of God we will live in condemnation day in and day out.

If memories of past sins persist to haunt and accuse you, remember that you are forgiven. SAY OUT LOUD, "I am forgiven." Say it until you believe it and receive God's forgiveness. Do you believe Jesus has died for your sins? Have you given Him all your sins? Are you remaining accused of a sin you have confessed, or do you believe His death paid for your sins? The decision is yours. Jesus already decided to forgive you. It's up to you to receive it. Don't let these memories accuse you. He has forgiven you, forgive yourself.

Jesus received the full punishment for every sin we committed, those past, present, and future, so you don't have to. Remember, there is no sin too big for God except the one you keep. But why keep it if Jesus already died to take it? There is no sin Jesus can't handle so give it to Him, confess it, and be done with it. You may sin again tomorrow, but let's trust God with all our tomorrows too. When we accept his forgiveness, we accept his Son's death and then Jesus didn't die in vain.

> **Galatians 2:21** *"I do not nullify the grace of God, for if righteousness comes through the Law, then Christ died needlessly."*

Little ole us. We have to believe He loves us as much as anyone else. He has no favorites, and we are his most prized possession. Choose to believe you are worth dying for and don't let those memories haunt you.

6

ARE YOU NERVOUS?

Are you worried about your children? Worry, fear, and nervousness are simply a lack of faith. This is not to condemn you but to give you hope. I say this to free you! When I get nervous, it helps me to realize that my faith in God to come through for my family or for me has gone right out the window.

Fear and nervousness are the opposite of Faith. When we are nervous about something, we are trusting in ourselves to pull us through instead of God. We never have confidence in ourselves, which is why we are always nervous.

If you are worried about your children, you are not trusting God to draw them and guide them as He has promised. This should be liberating because we believe in a God that loves our children even more than we do. I am not saying we aren't supposed to teach them and raise them and intervene when necessary. What I am saying is fear and worry are not supposed to be a regular part of life. Worrying about a child does not mean you love them more. I think many of us grew up believing worry was a normal part of life, especially parenthood.

I can become consumed with worry. Are my children being corrupted by friends; are they choosing to drink/do drugs/have sex; are they being seduced; are they watching too much television/phone/video games? My children are in college and the workforce. My influence, though real, is not as effective as it once was. I have to trust God.

Worry is misplaced faith. Worry is meditating on what could happen, the worst possible outcome, and what ifs. I can quickly be consumed with what may happen instead of being overwhelmed with the promises of God. What are you thinking about regarding your children? What are you saying about them to family members and friends? Does your worry shine through or does your trust in God to intervene shine through? Whose power are you leaning on? Whose power do you believe in?

> **Acts 16:31** *"And they said, 'Believe in the Lord Jesus and you and your household will be saved.'"*
>
> **Isaiah 44:3-4** *"I will pour out water upon the thirsty ground, streams upon the dry land; I will pour out My spirit upon your offspring, My blessing upon your descendants. They shall spring forth amid grass like poplars beside flowing waters."*
>
> **Isaiah 54:13** *"All your children shall be taught by the Lord; great shall be the peace of your children."*
>
> **Isaiah 59:21** *"And as for me, this is my covenant with them,"* says the LORD: *"My Spirit that is upon you, and My words that I have put in your mouth, shall not depart out of your mouth, or out of the mouth of your offspring, or out of the*

mouth of your children's offspring," says the LORD, "from this time forth and forevermore."

Psalms 102:28 *"The children of your servants shall dwell secure; their offspring shall be established before you."*

Acts 2:15-17 *"'And it shall come to pass in the last days,' says God, 'that I will pour out of My Spirit on all flesh; your sons and your daughters shall prophesy, your young men shall see visions.'"*

Are you ready to believe God's word and stand on it, lean on it? "The proof of the pudding is in the eating." The evidence is in your "confession," the words of your mouth, and the meditation of your heart.

TODAY say to yourself and others what God says regarding your children.

"My children are saved and wise and thoughtful. My children are not easily seduced or distracted. Jesus is their hope, and in Him, they rest; on Him, they rely. They are drawn to God. They know the difference between right and wrong and choose life. My children are filled with the Holy Spirit and are seeking God with all their heart, mind, and strength. They are courageous and bold and confident. They are successful in all they do because Jesus is their hope and on His words they feed."

Say this in faith. Believe this is God's plan for your children. Don't worry about whether or not it's true yet in the physical realm. Say it in faith. Faith is believing not in what we see but in God's truth. Believe like Abraham, who believed God could bring the dead back to life and create new things out of nothing. God expects us to believe He really is doing a work in those we are praying for.

> **Romans 4:17** *"He is our father in the sight of God, in whom he believed, who gives life to the dead and calls into being what does not exist."*

Are you praying for your children to be saved? Are you praying for them to be filled with wisdom? If so, then start declaring it! Don't wait until you see it. Believe it is done. That is faith. Faith is believing before you see it.

7

GENERATIONAL STRONGHOLDS

Some strongholds are passed down through generations. Negative thought patterns, if not dealt with, are passed down from father to son, mother to daughter, grandfather to granddaughter, etc. Sin and strongholds may come to you through your ancestors, but they don't have to remain with you. Sin is sin, and anger and moodiness are still sins and must be dealt with. Jesus dealt with sin, your sin and your parent's sin, yesterday's sins, today's sins, and tomorrow's sins. Confess your sins. Do not live with them and tolerate them. We like to blame our ancestors because for some reason it makes us feel better, and also gives us permission to keep certain habits and sins. Sin is sin, whether you were born that way or not. Just because your lousy temper came from your ancestors, it is not a license to rage.

We say things like:

- It's just the way I am.

- God made me this way.
- Deal with it.

We say and think things like:

- It runs in my family.
- It's in my genes.
- We are Italian, after all.
- My mother had breast cancer and so did her mother before her.
- Everybody drinks in my family; we're Irish.
- I was born homosexual; it's just who I am.

Due to no fault of your own, you are prone to violence, moodiness, or rage. You may be naturally hot-tempered or shy. We like to say some people just have addictive personalities.

We may have been born with those tendencies, but we don't have to remain that way.

There is no way out if you think it is just the way you are. There is no forgiveness if you don't recognize sin as sin.

Is it ok to be moody or fly off the handle just because your ancestors are known for this?

Are you ready for some earthshaking, mind-blowing good news? If Jesus said we are born again, then we are born again, free of every generational curse that has been following us through our bloodline. If that is not good enough, there is more! It will not go any further. It stops with you. It will not be passed down to your children unless you let it, unless you accept it as "just the way it is." We have a new bloodline, a new and unique heritage, a new ancestry. We were born again and transferred into the kingdom of the Son where we are coheirs with Christ.

> **Ephesians 3:6** *"This mystery is that through the gospel the Gentiles are heirs together with Israel, members together of one body, and sharers together in the promise in Christ Jesus."*

Jesus says we are new creations.

> **2 Corinthians 5:17** *"If anyone is in Christ he is a new creation, the old has gone, the new has come."*

These aren't just words. This is the truth. God tells us that in Christ, we are brand new. In Him we are born again, new creations, molded and shaped in His image. You have the opportunity today to be the YOU God created YOU to be. God has you in His mind, and He is molding you into a noble, respectable, gracious, wise, pure, kind, generous, heroic, fine person of integrity with a heart for God.

You don't have to remain that timid, fearful, easily offended, critical, worried person anymore. You also do not have to stay trapped in sinful behavior. It is not "just the way you are." You are no longer that person.

> **Galatians 3:28-29** *"There is neither Jew nor Greek, slave nor free, male nor female, for you are all one in Christ Jesus. If you belong to Christ, then you are Abraham's seed, and heirs according to the promise."*

Are you ready for the cure? You are like DAVID, and these thoughts are like GOLIATH. Jesus said:

Luke 10:19 *"Behold, I have given you the power to tread upon serpents and scorpions and upon the full force of the enemy and nothing will harm you."*

Are you ready for success? Because SUCCESS is the new you. It was paid for, and I will show you how to live free and experience complete success and have a new life. The life you were meant to live. It's yours. You deserve it. If anyone deserves it, you do. YES, YOU! Stop listening to the liar, the accuser. Your ship has not sailed.

What if you have already passed down particularly unpleasant traits to your children? God is the God of the impossible. He can and will reverse any curse and cancel any stronghold. Nothing is too difficult for God. He is the God who was and is and is to come. He is beyond time. God is not bound by time or anything in this natural world. He created time and distance and He is master of the universe. God can heal your children and renew them. He can and will. There is no one God wants to leave in darkness or in the pit of despair. There is no one God wants prone to sin or cursed with character flaws. He restores, renews, cleanses, wipes clean, and completely forgives and recreates us in His image. Watch Him do a work on you and yours. Believe big. God hears a parent's prayer for a child. Believe it.

John 14:11-14 *"Amen, amen, I say to you, whoever believes in Me will do the works that I do, and will do greater ones than these, because I am going to the Father. And whatever you ask in My name, I will do, so that the Father may be glorified in the Son. If you ask anything of Me in My name, I will do it."*

For more on how to pray go to "TOOLS FOR THE BATTLE - PRAYER"

8

YOU ARE PRECIOUS TO GOD

God doesn't love you more today than He did yesterday, nor will He love you more tomorrow than He does today. God doesn't love you more when you are good and less when you are bad. He will never love you any more or less than He does right now.

God's mind about you will never change. No matter what you do or don't do. He has made up His mind about you, and His mind will not change. He is not like us. He is not easily swayed or moody, nor does He make hasty decisions.

He decided to send his Son to the cross for you and me because we are worth it. There is nothing we can do to earn His love or drive His love away from us. He loves us knowing what we think and watching how we act. He knows what drives us and yet He loves us just the way we are.

We love conditionally, but God loves us unconditionally. When someone is bad, we treat them as if they are bad. We give them the silent treatment, or we reject them. But God is not like us. His standards are not our standards. His ways are not our ways.

We think God is like us, so we expect Him to act like we do. God is not human and therefore He never gets moody, nor does He ever get frustrated with us. He doesn't punish us to hurt us, He prunes us so we can grow bigger and better and lovelier. He always and ONLY has our best interest at heart. God is not out to get us or punish us, but only discipline us with love.

We were raised, some of us, to withhold love when a child is bad. But it doesn't have to be that way. It's not God's way. We can discipline and love at the same time. We can take away the phone and tell them we love them at the same time.

He didn't say, "Get your act together first and then I will love you; be good and then I will love you." He chose to love us whether we ever love Him back or not. He chose to love us as sinners. This is our God. He loves us, sin and all.

> **Romans 5:8** *"But God proves His love for us in that while we were still sinners Christ died for us."*

God proved His love for us by dying for us while we were still sinners. This was proof that He will always love us no matter what we do. God wants us to have faith in His love for us even when we sin. When we are sinful and following habits that are sinful, God wants us to remember that even in our sinfulness we can have faith in His love. We need to know that He hasn't skipped town or rejected us because we have sinned.

HAVE FAITH IN HIS LOVE FOR YOU. Believe He loves you. Give this to God as a gift. Quit insulting Him with your doubt. Quit doubting His love when He has already proven it. If Jesus taking the cross for you won't prove His love for you then nothing will. NOTHING.

While we were still sinners, He died for us. He demonstrated His love for us. Once and for all. There is nothing else He can do to convince us that He loves us. What else can He do? What will it take to prove to us that He loves us? What does He have to do?

> **Romans 5:7-8** *"Very rarely will anyone die for a righteous person, though for a good person someone might possibly dare to die. But God proves His love for us in that while we were still sinners Christ died for us."*

A woman came to me for prayer; I will call her "Mary." I ended up praying with her for months and months and often daily. She was seeking GOD. She was desperate for His love. She told me on many occasions that she wanted to end her life. Mary just couldn't believe that God loved her after all she had done. She desperately wanted to believe in His love for her. I think to this day that her desperation for God's love drove her to bombard me until she believed.

Mary told me how when she was just a young girl, she wished a friend of hers would die and said it to her face. The girl died that very day and Mary held on to the guilt her whole life. She thought she was responsible for the girl's death and sold her soul to the devil not long afterward. She thought there was no hope for her and that she had gone too far. She thought she was forever doomed.

As she was telling me this, I heard from the Holy Spirit that she was believing a lie she had heard from a movie. Movies do a lot of damage. In movies, we learn that if you sell your soul to the devil, there is no hope for you. There is no going back. This is just not true. Through Jesus Christ and His infinite mercy, there is always hope. It's never too late.

Once someone asked me, "How do I know I am saved ?" I was praying in the Holy Spirit, and the answer practically flew out of my mouth, "Because Jesus does the saving and He does a good job."

JESUS SAVES, and He does it well. We just have to believe it and rest in that fact. Guess who saves the lost? Jesus. Jesus saves the lost, not the lost. They are lost, and the lost cannot save themselves. Jesus saves you and me. He came to save us, all of us. That was His mission. His mission is you and me and all who need saving. He saves those who are lost. He doesn't save those who don't need saving, only those who know they are lost and come to Him.

How do I know He still loves me? This question plagues people. People want to know. "Mary" asked me the same question. "How do I know God loves me?"

I finally told her just receive His love for His sake. You owe it to God to believe He loves you. He gave Jesus for you. There is nothing more He can do to prove He loves you. He can't send Jesus to die for you again. How many times does Jesus have to go to the cross for you to believe He loves you? He came once for all!!!! You are part of that "ALL," just believe it and receive His love. He has already given His love. You have to accept it. He already died for you; He isn't planning on dying again for you, He has already done it. He already decided for you. He loves you. PERIOD. Just quit doubting.

I told Mary, "He loves us even when we sin. He proved it by sending His son to us while we were still sinners." Finally, I just lifted my hand in the air, and said, "Do this. Say, 'Lord, I choose to believe you love me whether You do or don't love me. I choose to believe You do and may it be my gift to you. Whether or not You love me is Your problem, God. I am going to believe You do, as my gift to You."

If God gave His Son for us because He loves us and for no other reason, then don't you think the greatest gift we can give God is to receive His gift?

If you were the only person on Earth, God would have sent His Son to die just for you. That is how much He loves and cherishes you.

Why do we doubt His love for us? We do! If we were really honest with ourselves, we would realize just how unsure we are of His love and devotion to us. We doubt He will be with us when we need Him; we doubt we will be taken care of in our old age. We doubt, but God demands our faith in His love for us. Have faith in His love. God wants you to believe and trust in His love for you. It's not enough to believe God exists. God expects us to believe not just that He exists, even the devil believes that, but that He loves us unconditionally. He went to great lengths to prove His love.

God proved He loved us by sending Jesus to die in our place. What an act of love! He did it so you and I would never doubt His love for us. Yet we doubt. If God sending His Son to die doesn't prove to you that He loves you, then nothing will. Some might give their life for a noble purpose or for a special loved one, but God sent Jesus to die for us while we were sinners, proving His love for us. He didn't wait for us to

get our act together. No, He didn't. He loves you and He
loves me just the way we are.

9

YOUR WORTH

W e are worth everything to Him. The fact that God loves us, sins and all, is what makes God so special. He already chose you and me. He chose us to be His children before time began. Establish this forever in your head. YOU ARE LOVED and worth everything to God.

> **Ephesians 1:4** *"As he chose us in him, before the foundation of the world."*

He didn't wait to see what we would be like before He chose us and decided to send His Son to die for us. He already knows us and wants us, sins and all. He decided to send His son knowing we were sinful. It's so hard for us to believe because we would be so different if we were God. God's ways are not our ways. There is nothing you can do to change His mind about you. He already made up His mind when He sent Jesus to die for you. He loved you before you were born. He loved you before you could earn His love. God sacrificed Jesus so He could have us.

NOW LISTEN TO THIS! God sacrificed His only Son without any assurance anyone would accept this sacrifice. He sacrificed Jesus knowing many would not even notice or care. God was willing to give His Son Jesus even if no one chose to receive His gift. That's how valuable you are to Him. God has determined our value: we are priceless to Him. Your value is equal to Jesus according to God. If God is willing to give up Jesus for you, you must be extremely valuable to God. You are priceless and God proved it by sending Jesus to die in your place.

> **1 Peter 1:18-19** *"Realizing that you were ransomed from your futile conduct, handed on by your ancestors, not with perishable things like silver or gold but with the precious blood of Christ as of a spotless unblemished lamb."*

You were bought, purchased, redeemed, ransomed. Your salvation wasn't cheap. God paid for your freedom. He didn't have to, but you matter that much to Him. Stop trying to figure out who you are; you are already someone special in God's eyes. Stop trying to figure out your value; you are already valuable. ASK GOD who you are and what you are worth to Him.

> I say this because most of us determine our value incorrectly. We do not know our value. The value we place on ourselves depends on how we feel on any particular day and it depends on what others think of us. If we were to place a value on ourselves it would go up and down, but God established our worth forever. It is established forever. The value he places on you never changes.

When someone tells us we are ugly or worthless, we believe them. We feel worthless and ugly. We see ourselves worthless and ugly. Stop listening to the liar! Jesus called the devil a liar. He has been lying to the human race since he lied to Adam and Eve in the Garden of Eden. He lied to them, and they believed him. God said, "Eat this one particular fruit from this one particular tree, and you will die." The devil, in the form of a snake said, "You will certainly not die." They believed the devil. Adam and Eve believed the words of a snake over God. We do the same thing. We believe what the world says about how we should look and what we should like. Imagine how we would feel if we didn't care what ignorant fools say about us, but only about what the God of the Universe says about us.

God's mind about you is made up! Nothing can change His mind regarding you. He is unchanging; He doesn't change His mind about us because we sin or forget about Him. He doesn't love us because of our goodness or our abilities; He just loves us because we are His. God cannot love you any more than He does at this very moment. God does not love you more if you do good deeds or less if you fail to. There is nothing you can do to earn His love; just receive it. God cannot love you any less than He does right now. He doesn't love you more or less based on your behavior or actions. He doesn't love you less when you sin, no matter how grievous. This is called unconditional love. We don't understand it. It's foreign to us. His unconditional love is the basis for all love and the reason we can love and forgive. To forgive it takes unconditional love, the love of the Father.

There is no getting away from Him. There is nothing that can separate us from Him because we are in Jesus Christ. Jesus took away the sin that separates us from God. Jesus came between God and us with the cross, and through Him, we have an open door to the throne room of God.

> **John 15:13** *"There is no greater love than to lay down one's life for one's friends."*

> **John 3:16** *"For God so loved the world that he gave his one and only Son, that whoever believes in Him shall not perish but have eternal life."*

Today is the day we begin to undo all the lies. Jesus said in **John 8:44** *"You belong to your father, the devil, and you want to carry out your father's desires. He was a murderer from the beginning, not holding to the truth, for there is no truth in him. When he lies, he speaks his native language, for he is a liar and the father of lies."*

The devil is happy to tell you who you are. Stop listening. He will say to you; you are too tall, too short, too fat, too loud, too ugly, too mean, and just too bad. He will tell you, you are stuck, and your life is over. Stop listening and believing his lies.

God gave me a word for you today. He wants you to hear who you are, who you really are.

- You are, according to God, unshakable and forever enduring, like a mountain (Psalm 127:1).
- You are holy and sanctified (1 Cor. 1:2).
- You are forgiven (Romans 8:2),
- righteous and wise (1 Cor. 1:30).
- You are knowledgeable (1 Cor. 1:5)
- and blessed (Galatians 3:14).

- You are established, anointed and triumphant (2 Cor. 1:21, 2:14).
- You are strong in the Lord (Ephesians 6:10).
- You are brand new in Christ, fearfully and wonderfully made (2 Cor 5:17, Psalm 139:14).
- Because of Christ you can move mountains, heal the sick, and cast out demons (Mark 11:23, Mark 16:17).
- You are an overcomer, nothing is too difficult for you (Romans 8:37, Phil 4:13).
- You are full of the Holy Spirit and signs and wonders follow you. Jesus said you will do greater things than he did because He is going to the Father and whatever you ask in His name He will do (John 14:13).

THIS IS YOU. The devil will lead you to sin continually because he wants you to doubt this! The devil wants you to question yourself and feel unqualified. The devil wants you feeling forever unworthy. The devil wants you unstable and always wondering if you are good enough. He wants you to care about what others think of you instead of what God thinks of you.

We don't walk by faith in what the devil says.

We don't walk by feelings. We walk by faith, believing in the complete forgiveness and love and mercy and grace of God. That is what faith is. Faith is believing in God's love and forgiveness. Faith is believing God loves us, even in our sinful state.

You are anointed. You are the hands and feet of Christ. God has given you everything you need, including His very self, to minister to God's people. The devil, however, will try to keep us on the sidelines focusing on ourselves and our faults. When we look at ourselves, we see our weaknesses and everything we can't do or don't deserve to do. We see everything that disqualifies us and keeps us from working for God's Kingdom, especially from the ability to help others or serve God. Instead, we need to see ourselves as God sees us, forgiven, delivered, redeemed!

Turn your eyes to Jesus. Read His word and what He has to say to you today. He will restore you and your faith. He is the one who qualifies us. He is our source. We are unqualified. We are all unqualified. The Bible says we are all lost, sick, and sinful without Him. He makes us good, healthy, whole, repaired, restored, and clean. He is the SOURCE, was the SOURCE, and will always be the SOURCE, today, yesterday, and forever.

Did you lose your cool today? You are not disqualified. God still needs you. Rise and walk right now!

Did you strike out at someone, maybe gossip or feel hatred toward a family member or friend? You are not disqualified. Get back up and ask for forgiveness and rise and walk right now.

Moping and wallowing in guilt and shame is worthless and a waste unless it leads you to repentance. Let it bring you to repentance right now and then stand up. STAND UP, NOW. Thinking about it won't help you. Jesus will. Go to Him now. Let the Holy Spirit lead you and teach you and show you what to do.

You are anointed (called) to bring good news, to comfort those who mourn, save the lost, heal the broken-hearted, set the prisoners free and to declare the salvation of our Lord (see Isaiah 61:1). If not you, who? Someone perfect? Stand up, get up off the floor, dust yourself off, and remind yourself who you are.

REPEAT THESE I AM'S

- I am strong in the Lord and in His mighty power.
- I am loved, and I am forgiven.
- I am made whole, healed, and completely restored because Jesus died for me.
- I am a child of the most High God.
- I am precious to him.
- I am highly favored and the joy of my Father in heaven.
- I am royalty and heir to God's kingdom.
- I am the salt of the earth and the light of the world according to Jesus and can do all things through Christ.
- I am victorious over sin and no longer ruled and driven by sin or addictions.
- I am free and an overcomer.
- The Holy Spirit lives in me, and I follow Him.
- I choose Christ.

Say this every day, especially when you are down and out.

10

SOMEONE HAD TO DIE

Someone had to die. Jesus didn't just happen to get trapped and crucified. He went to the cross for us. Jesus wasn't defeated, He was the aggressor. He came to defeat the enemy. He had a purpose. He came to die for us, to destroy the curse against us and all the work of the devil. He came, and He conquered. He fought and won. He won at the cross. The war against sin and sickness and darkness was won when Jesus died on the cross and rose from the dead. Jesus paid the price and we reap the rewards.

The Bible says, "the wages of sin is death" (Romans 6:23). You sin, you die. In the Garden God told Adam and Eve, if you eat the fruit of the Tree of Knowledge, you will certainly die. They died a spiritual death that day and along with them, the whole human race. God and sin do not mix. God is a loving God, but also a just God. The only way we can be free from sin is for someone to DIE in our place. Jesus brought us back to life by dying for us. He took the punishment (death) meant for us, so we could live with Him forever.

Romans 6:23 *"For the wages of sin is death, but the gift of God is eternal life in Christ Jesus our Lord."*

Jesus became the sacrificial Lamb of God for us because He really and truly loves us. That is why we call Him the Lamb of God. In the Old Testament, an altar was erected in the Tabernacle that Moses built according to God's instructions. On the altar, day and night, sacrifices were made for the sins of the people. Lambs and bulls and goats were slaughtered, and the blood of the animals was poured out on the altar and covered the sins of the people. These animals died in place of the people.

These sacrifices were a foreshadowing of the true Lamb of God that was coming to take away the sins of the world. Jesus is the lamb that was slain for us, and His blood went into the "MOST HOLY PLACE," heaven, where Jesus himself, our high priest, presented to God the Father, His very own blood, as the atoning sacrifice for the sins of the world. God accepted Jesus' gift of Himself; God accepted Jesus' blood in exchange for our lives. On earth, the high priest offered a sacrifice for the sins of the nation. This was just a foreshadowing of the real offering to come. Jesus is our high priest. He is both the priest and the offering. He offers Himself not on a human altar; not on the one made with human hands. No, He presented himself and His blood to God Himself in heaven.

Hebrews 9:22 *"According to the law almost everything is purified by blood, and without the shedding of blood there is no forgiveness."*

Jesus is the true Lamb of God. God required not just any lamb from the people but the unblemished lambs. God expected the best from the people. This, too, was a foreshadowing of Jesus, who was the only one who could keep the law and truly be an unblemished offering for the sins of the people. He was sinless and, therefore, the perfect Lamb of God, the perfect, unblemished Lamb.

When He sacrificed Himself for us, He not only took our sins from us but exchanged natures with us. He became sin so we could become righteous. He did not just take sin away but changed us. He gave us a new nature, a righteous nature.

> **2 Corinthians 5:21** *"For our sake He made Him to be sin who did not know sin, so that we might become the righteousness of God in him."*

> **2 Corinthians 5:17** *"So whoever is in Christ is a new creation: the old things have passed away; behold, new things have come."*

This is very important. The Bible doesn't say that Jesus just took our sins, it goes much further and tells us that he became sin. THIS IS HUGE and of the utmost importance. I hope you get this. Jesus wants us to know that he became something so we could become something. He didn't just give us righteous acts or the ability to do righteous things. He gave us a new nature, a righteous nature. He became sin so we could become righteous. He wants us to get this. He wants us to see ourselves cleansed and righteous. We tend to be always striving and trying to get somewhere and become something, when He wants us to know we are already there. We are already somebody new.

The Bible says it again in Romans.

> **5:19** *"For just as through the disobedience of one person the many were made sinners, so through the obedience of one the many will be made righteous."*

He gave us new hearts, hearts cleansed, hearts that long for Him and hearts that want to do His will. Jesus really did do it all for us. He even gave us what it takes to love Him and follow Him and obey Him. Be patient with yourself. God is working in you to move you to follow Him and obey Him. Just don't quit Him.

> **Ezekiel 36:26** *"I will give you a new heart, and a new spirit I will put within you. I will remove the heart of stone from your flesh and give you a heart of flesh."*

We are new creations. We are spirit, soul, and body, and while our spirit is brand new and alive, our mind, will, and emotions (soul) need to be renewed daily. We genuinely become brand new when we choose Him for ourselves. Our parents may have accepted Christ for us when we were baptized, but at some point, we have to choose Him for ourselves. This is when everything changes. The seed planted in you at baptism comes to life when you choose Christ for yourself. Consequently, taking the Eucharist becomes a brand new, life-changing experience.

> **2 Corinthians 5:17-21** *"Consequently, from now on we regard no one according to the flesh; even if we once knew Christ according to the flesh, yet now we know him so no longer. [17] So whoever is in Christ is a new creation: the old things have passed away; behold, new things have come. [18] And all this is*

from God, who has reconciled us to Himself through Christ and given us the ministry of reconciliation, [19] namely, God was reconciling the world to Himself in Christ, not counting their trespasses against them and entrusting to us the message of reconciliation. [20] So we are ambassadors for Christ, as if God were appealing through us. We implore you on behalf of Christ, be reconciled to God. [21] For our sake He made him to be sin who did not know sin, so that we might become the righteousness of God in him."

Jesus became sin for us and took the cross that He didn't deserve, so we could become right with God and receive life and all the blessings God intended for us. He didn't deserve the cross, and we don't deserve righteousness. Every time we try to earn righteousness, it is a slap in Jesus' face, who gave it to us as a gift. He earned it for us. We get what Jesus earned for us.

God gave Israel the Law to obey, promising them life and blessings if they observed ALL He commanded. If they chose to obey God, they would be blessed by God.

Deuteronomy 28:2 *"All these blessings will come upon you and overwhelm you when you obey the voice of the Lord, your God."*

If they chose not to obey, they would be cursed.

Deuteronomy 28:15 *"But it shall come to pass, if you do not obey the voice of the Lord your God, to observe carefully all His commandments and His statutes which I command you today, that all these curses will come upon you and overtake you."*

God, knowing we could not keep His commandments, made a way for us to gain every blessing promised in the Old Testament. Jesus obeyed for us. Jesus is God's gift to us, the gift that brings life and blessings.

> **Galatians 3:13–14** *"Christ ransomed us from the curse of the law by becoming a curse for us, for it is written, "Cursed be everyone who hangs on a tree," that the blessing of Abraham might be extended to the Gentiles through Christ Jesus, so that we might receive the promise of the Spirit through faith."*

Read **Deuteronomy 28:1–14** to learn about the blessings of obedience Jesus earned for us by His obedience unto death. Read from **Deuteronomy 28:15** to the end of the book to learn of the curses for disobedience Jesus took for us. He took the full brunt for us.

The Bible says, *"There is therefore now no condemnation to those who are in Christ Jesus, who do not walk according to the flesh, but according to the Spirit"* (**Romans 8:1**). The Bible does **NOT** say that there is now no condemnation for those who are perfect.

Today we come boldly to GOD the Father through Jesus Christ. We come boldly and confidently because our hope is not in what we have done but in what Jesus has done. This is why we come in confidence. We have no confidence coming in our own strength or goodness. That will always fail us or betray us. But Jesus was perfect, and He perfectly fulfilled every commandment for us. He gave us His perfection. He gave us His right to enter the Holy of Holies. He gave us what He earned, not what we deserve. He did it all for us.

Jesus loves you so much that He died for you. He died for you, so let it count. Don't let Jesus' death on the cross be in vain. Let Him take ALL your sins because He wants them, and we were not meant to carry them. The price He paid for you is beyond measure because you are worth everything to HIM. Don't rob Jesus of YOU. You are His reward — His prize for taking the cross. He won the battle, and the battle was for us. We, you and I, are God's gift to Jesus. If we hold onto our sins and refuse the forgiveness Jesus won for us, we are saying He died in vain, and He shouldn't have bothered to die.

11

FORGIVE YOURSELF

Have you received God's forgiveness? Have you forgiven yourself? Are your sins on you or on Christ Jesus? He died to take your sins. His death had a purpose to restore you to a right relationship with God.

Is Jesus your savior? Did He take your sins from you? Have you forgiven yourself? Are your sins too big for Jesus? Are they too ugly, too horrible for Jesus? If this is the case, what will it take to get your sins forgiven? If Jesus isn't the answer, what is? Is there something you feel you have to do? Do you feel as if you still have to pay something? Jesus paid it for you. He paid it all. There is nothing left to pay.

NOTHING. If you still think you have to earn forgiveness then you are rejecting His mercy and grace. He offers us mercy and grace. If you still feel something is required from you to be forgiven then you are telling God the Father, who sent His Son to the cross for your sins, that it wasn't good enough. He should have done more. If we still have to do something on our own, then Christ died for nothing.

Galatians 2:21 *"I do not nullify the grace of God; for if justification comes through the law, then Christ died for nothing."*

God decided Jesus' death on the cross accomplished salvation for all who call on His name. You can accept it or reject it. This is salvation. Not everyone wants to accept this gift. Those who reject Jesus and His death are telling God He shouldn't have bothered. Jesus died in vain. If you believe your sins are on you, then what was the purpose of Jesus dying on the cross?

It is a sin to remain unforgiven. We say, "I just can't forgive myself." We say it as if it's something to be proud of. It sounds so noble, "I can't forgive myself. I will never forgive myself," as if it is a pious, humble thing to say. It's still a sin. God does not feel sorry for you.

Unforgiveness is a sin. It means you have decided Jesus' death was too much for your sin. You are really saying His death was meaningless. He should never have bothered. He should never have been crucified. Any time you carry your sins you are saying that your sins are too big and bad for Jesus. You are saying, in effect, that God didn't know what He was doing when He sent Jesus to the earth to die for us. Jesus died in vain.

Isaiah 43:25 *"I, even I, am He who blots out your transgressions for my own sake, and remembers your sins no more."*

Don't bother reminding God about a sin He has already chosen to forget. You may keep remembering it, but God has chosen to forget it. That sin doesn't bother him anymore. It has been forgiven; dealt with.

Psalm 103:12 *"As far as the east is from the west, so far has he removed our sins from us."*

How can God feel sorry for you if He has already forgiven you? If you remain in a state of sorrow, guilt, and shame, then you don't believe He forgave you. We can accept the fact that we are forgiven in Christ, or we can believe the devil's lie that we are still guilty and should, therefore, feel guilty.

God has done everything for you. There is nothing He won't do for you. You are His child. The Bible says if He gave Jesus for you, there is nothing He won't do. Take the forgiveness that Jesus offered to the world when He died for you.

Romans 8:31 *"What then shall we say to this? If God is for us, who can be against us? ³² He who did not spare his own Son but handed him over for us all, how will he not also give us everything else along with him?"*

12

ONCE UPON A TIME

ONCE UPON A TIME in the 4th century AD, in Korea, a man had two sons. The elder rose to become Chief Justice in the land and the younger became an infamous bandit. The elder brother loved his younger brother but was unable to persuade him to change his ways.

Eventually, the younger son was caught and brought before his brother, the Chief Justice. Everyone in the courtroom thought the younger brother would get off because it was well known that the Chief Justice loved his brother, but at the end of the trial, the Chief Justice sentenced his brother to death.

On the day of the execution, the elder brother came to the prison and said to his brother, "Let's swap places." The younger brother agreed, thinking that once they realized that it was the elder brother, the execution would not go forward.

On he went up on the hill to watch the proceedings. His brother was brought out at dawn and, to his horror, executed. Filled with remorse, he ran down the hill and told the guard his name and that he was the criminal who should be executed. The guards said to him, "There is no sentence outstanding on anyone with that name."

This is the case for those who choose Christ. There is no sentence outstanding. Our sins have been done away with.

Isaiah 1:18 *"Come now, let us set things right, says the Lord: Though your sins be like scarlet, they may become white as snow; Though they be red like crimson, they may become white as wool."*

1 John 1:9 *"If we acknowledge our sins, He is faithful and just and will forgive our sins and cleanse us from every wrongdoing."*

Psalm 103:12 *"As far as the east is from the west, so far has he removed our sins from us.*

"

13

HEALING

Matthew 8:7 *Jesus said to him, "I will go and heal him."*

Jesus heals. He healed 2000 years ago and He is still healing now. If you were to take all the Gospels out of the Bible and stack them up on top of each other and then cut out all the healings and deliverances, you wouldn't have much of a stack left. It is God's nature to heal. It is His privilege, His joy, and His desire to heal His children.

What good mother or father would let their children remain sick? Our joy as parents is to be the one that makes it better; the one that makes the fever go away, or the flu. "Let Daddy kiss it and make it better." The same is true of our Father in heaven.

> Matthew 7:9-11 *"Which one of you would hand his son a stone when he asks for a loaf of bread, or a snake when he asks for a fish? If you then, who are wicked, know how to give good gifts to your children, how much more will your heavenly Father give good things to those who ask Him?"*

Matthew 7:7–8 *"Ask, and it will be given to you; seek, and you will find; knock, and it will be opened to you. For everyone who asks receives, and he who seeks finds, and to him who knocks it will be opened."*

Ask, and you WILL receive, the Bible says. It doesn't say you may receive, it says you will. But you have to ask in faith.

Mark 11:24 *"Therefore I tell you, whatever you ask for in prayer, believe that you have received it, and it will be yours."*

Jesus doesn't mince words. He says what He means and He means what He says. It just seems to us too good to be true, so we just choose to doubt. I want to encourage you to go beyond what you have accepted as the truth and dare to believe. Enter into faith with me as we go through these next pages. Dare to believe there is more for you than you are experiencing or have ever experienced before. Dare to believe these words from the Bible are true and for you.

John 14:13 *"And whatever you ask in my name, I will do, so that the Father may be glorified in the Son. You may ask Me for anything in My name and I will do it."*

Jesus said we can ask the Father for anything and when we do, He says He will do whatever we ask! Jesus' heart's desire is to glorify the Father. He wants the world to know how good His father is and to believe in Him. Jesus wants everyone to see how awesome and wonderful the Father is. It is through you and me that the Father is glorified. When we pray and receive an answer to our prayer, we too, with Jesus, can glorify God and praise His holy name! We will want to share the good news and testify about what God has done.

> **Matthew 18 :19-20** *"Again, amen I say to you, if two of you agree on earth about anything for which they are to pray, it shall be granted to them by My heavenly father. For where two or three are gathered together in My name, there am I in the midst of them."*

> **Hebrews 4:16** *"Let us then approach the Throne of Grace with confidence so that we may receive mercy and find grace to help us in our time of need."*

Jesus let Himself be crucified so the veil would be torn that separated us from God the Father. Jesus wants us to ask so God can give. We were given the right to access God Almighty through the name of Jesus. We were given the privilege to enter the throne room of Grace through the blood of Jesus, through faith in His name. He wants us to come to Him, not in fear or begging, but in faith and with confidence knowing our Father desires this for us.

> **Isaiah 53:5** *"But He was pierced for our transgressions, He was crushed for our iniquities; the punishment that brought us peace was on Him, and by His wounds we are healed."*

> **Matthew 8:16-17** *"When it was evening, they brought him many who were possessed by demons, and he drove out the spirits by a word and cured all the sick, to fulfill what had been said by Isaiah the prophet: 'He took away our infirmities and bore our diseases.'"*

Jesus heals today just like yesterday. He hasn't changed. He is still alive and sitting at the right hand of God, forever interceding on our behalf. As a matter of fact, Jesus never said no to anyone. Everyone was healed who asked Him or came to Him for healing.

God wants to heal you. I can say that until I am blue in the face, but you must read the Word of God, with the help of the Holy Spirit, to see this for yourself. Faith is believing God wants to heal you. Faith, the Bible says, comes from hearing God's word (Romans 10:17).

I used to have this plaque in my home above the door that read, "Faith is not believing God can, but that God will." Anyone can believe God can. It doesn't require faith to believe God can; even the devil believes God is able. Faith is required to believe He will. HE WILL! He wants to heal you more than you want to be healed. It is His will to heal you. Mark 1:41 should put this to rest for you.

> **Mark 1:40-42** *"A leper came to him, and kneeling down, begged Him and said, "If You wish, You can make me clean." Moved with pity, He stretched out His hand, touched him, and said to him, "I do will it. Be made clean." The leprosy left him immediately, and he was made clean."*

God isn't thinking about whether or not He should heal you every time you get sick. He has already made up His mind to heal you. You are the one who has trouble believing you are worthy of healing. We still think we have to earn healing and forgiveness.

There was a woman in the Bible who was sick for 12 years. Here is her story.

Mark 5:25-33 *There was a woman who had suffered terribly from severe bleeding for twelve years, 26 even though she had been treated by many doctors. She had spent all her money, but instead of getting better she got worse all the time. 27 She had heard about Jesus, so she came in the crowd behind him, 28 saying to herself, "If I just touch his clothes, I will get well." She touched his cloak, and her bleeding stopped at once; and she had the feeling inside herself that she was healed of her trouble. 30 At once Jesus knew that power had gone out of him, so he turned around in the crowd and asked, "Who touched my clothes?" His disciples answered, "You see how the people are crowding you; why do you ask who touched you?" But Jesus kept looking around to see who had done it. 33 The woman realized what had happened to her, so she came, trembling with fear, knelt at his feet, and told him the whole truth. 34 Jesus said to her, "My daughter, your faith has made you well. Go in peace, and be healed of your trouble."*

Be like this woman. Her faith healed her. What kind of faith did she have? Was it extraordinary? What did her faith look like? She simply believed Jesus would heal her if she just touched the hem of his garment. Jesus said, "Woman, your faith has made you well." Her faith was merely to believe He desired to heal her. That was her faith. That was all it took. Just believe He wants to heal you and Jesus will look at you and declare the same to you. "Son/Daughter, your faith has made you well." Faith isn't coming to Jesus with 10 pages of scripture memorized or attending Mass every day of the week. Faith is believing He will heal you.

Betsy, while kneeling before Jesus during adoration was explaining to Jesus that she was there for healing. She told Him that she knew that if she could just touch the edge of his robe, like the woman in this story, she would be healed! As she was saying the words, it hit her, "Jesus lives inside me! THE EDGE OF HIS ROBE IS INSIDE OF ME! Now then, how to touch that hem?"

With Faith!

We can touch his hem with faith! Our faith is how we touch His hem. My friend, Betsy, asked Jesus to increase her faith. Jesus recognized the woman's faith and Jesus will recognize your faith as well. Jesus wants to heal you too. He isn't thinking about it. He has already made up His mind.

One day a Roman soldier came to Jesus and asked him to heal his servant. He told Jesus that his servant was lying at home paralyzed and suffering dreadfully. Jesus said to him, "I will come and cure him." The soldier said in reply, "Lord, I am not worthy to have you enter under my roof; only say the word and my servant will be healed. For I too am a person subject to authority, with soldiers subject to me. And I say to one, 'Go,' and he goes; and to another, 'Come here,' and he comes; and to my slave, 'Do this,' and he does it." [10] When Jesus heard this, he was amazed and said to those following him, "Amen, I say to you, in no one in Israel have I found such faith. (Matthew 8:6-10 NABRE)

This soldier was not a Jew. He knew he had no right to ask such a thing from Jesus, but he did for the sake of his servant. How bold are you willing to be? Don't just ask, ask in faith. Jesus was amazed at this man's faith. Amaze Jesus with your faith.

God wants to heal you more than you want Him to heal you.

One night as I was praying, I began to pray for a young friend who was struggling with sickness. I told God, "Lord,

let me have it because I know how to fight this devil..."
before I could finish, I heard God say, "Me too! I too want to
take her place." I about freaked when the enormity of what
He said occurred to me. WOW. Jesus loves us so much He
took our place. He said to God, "Father, give it to Me, I know
I can handle it." Jesus loves us so much He died for all of us.

Jesus loves you and me so much He stood in our place and
received all our sins and sicknesses. He wanted to. He
wanted to take our place because He knew He could do it. I
was foolish to think I could take her place. Jesus did it. He
already did it. He wants us to just believe it. Let Jesus be
glorified. Let Jesus take it and get all the credit. He deserves
it for what he did for us.

Listen to what Peter says to the people right after the lame
man was healed in Acts chapter three.

> **Acts 3:12** *"You Israelites, why are you amazed at this, and why
> do you look so intently at us as if we had made him walk by our
> own power or piety?"*

It's not **your power or piety** that heals. PRAISE GOD. We
can never be holy enough to deserve healing. We can never
be holy enough to heal others. It is not our piety or "holiness" that heals. If it were we would get the glory. Imagine
how we would boast. We would be able to tell everyone,
"Come to me for healing." It is not our holiness that heals
but the Holy One who heals through us.

You don't deserve healing; you are not good enough and
never will be, but thanks be to God it has nothing to do with
your goodness. Jesus is our sanctification, our righteousness;
He is the one who makes us holy. Everything we are and

everything we deserve is because He earned it for us on the cross. He deserves all the glory.

Healing is a gift from God. Free. Just like forgiveness is a gift that cannot be earned, so is healing. God is merciful and forgiving. He doesn't show mercy to the deserving but the undeserving. Deserving people don't need mercy, they get what they deserve or earn. The undeserving get mercy and grace. You and I fall into this category. It can't be called mercy if we earn it. It can't be called grace if we have to do something for it. No, God is both gracious and merciful.

It takes faith to believe you are worthy of God's mercy and grace.

God's will is to heal you today, tomorrow, and always. God's will is to heal everyone.

> **Romans 8:31-32** *"What then shall we say to this? If God is for us, who can be against us? He who did not spare his own Son but handed him over for us all, how will He not also give us everything else along with Him?"*

If God were willing to give us His son, then he would provide us with anything. If He gave us Jesus, His best and most precious gift, He won't refuse us anything. If He didn't keep Jesus from us; He won't keep healing from us either. Don't doubt that God's will is to heal you. It always is.

> **Matthew 7:11** *"If you, though you are evil, know how to give good gifts to your children, how much MORE will your heavenly Father give good gifts to his children who ask him?"*

God does not love anyone else more than you. He has plenty of love and healing to go around. If He healed one, He heals all, so why not you? God doesn't pick and choose to heal some and not others. We are all the same in God's eyes. No one is more or less worthy. God does not have favorites.

If we don't believe God wants to heal everyone, all the time, then we will never believe He wants to heal us. In our minds, we will always be the one He doesn't heal. We will look at ourselves and our faults and always find a reason we don't deserve to be healed. If He were to heal some and not others, we would always see ourselves as the ones He doesn't heal.

Why would we deserve it more than someone else? We would always put ourselves in the "not healed" category because we will always find something about us that doesn't deserve to be healed. If God measured out healing based on merit, we would all fail. None of us would be worthy. Thank God, it's a gift attached to His work on the cross. GIVEN. DONE!!!

> **Matthew 8:16-17** "...he drove out the spirits by a word and cured all the sick, to fulfill what had been said by Isaiah the prophet: 'He took away our infirmities and bore our diseases.'"

God decided to heal you 2000 years ago when He sent Jesus, and He has not changed His mind. He made a decision to save you from your enemies when He sent Jesus to die on a cross. God rescued you from all evil and all darkness. And He has not changed His mind. He decided to forgive you and has not changed His mind. If there is sin keeping you from being healed, then receive forgiveness. Come to Jesus right now and be set free from whatever it is that prevents you from healing.

For more on Healing get my book "Be Healed in the Name of Jesus." https://www.spiritfilledcatholic.com/be-healed

My van was totaled when someone ran into me at a red light a few years back, so Mark (my husband) and I began to look for another car. The first car I entertained was a Ford Escape, but only briefly. I loved it but thought it wouldn't look as well as an Acura MDX in the "Middle School" carpool line.

I spent all my efforts on the MDX and kept coming up short. Many times, we made an appointment to see it, arrived at the dealership only to find it was already gone. We sat in parking lots looking at cars praying, "Lord, don't let us make a mistake. We want your will for us. You know what we need." We would be ready to decide on a vehicle, but feeling no peace, would leave.

Finally, one Friday morning Mark came up to me and said these words exactly, "Marybeth, I believe the reason we can't find a car is that God wants to give us one." I will never forget those words. That very evening on the way home from my son's baseball game, Mark said, "Do you want to go to Nissan of McKinney? They are raffling one of their cars tonight." I said, "Oh no, I have such a headache." He said, "They are giving away hotdogs and drinks."

I changed my mind and said, "YES."

On the way there we prayed, "Lord, if it's Your will, we are asking for favor in the raffle." I dropped Mark and David, my youngest son, off to fill out the paperwork, parked the car and caught up with David standing in line for hot dogs.

When I finally got a chance to look at the car they were raffling I said, "This is my car! THIS IS MY CAR!" It was a black Ford Escape with grey leather interior and side runners. It was perfect, and I loved it. When it was time for the raffle, they CHOSE OUR NAME. I sobbed thanking God. It was so obviously God. There was no doubt in our minds that night that this car was a gift from God.

If God cares about giving me a car, how much more does He care about my health? If He cares about me, He cares the same about you. He has no favorites. He loves us all the same. God is a good God and a giver. Expect to receive.

My friend, Pam Criss, shared this about her own experiences with healing.

> *"I say, ask God for everything — to take your headache away, for a good parking spot, to help your child ace the TAKS test, the raise you've been waiting for, etc., etc., etc. And be very specific in your prayer request so that you will genuinely KNOW that it's GOD who is answering. For example, don't just pray for marriages in general. Pray for your marriage and any marriage you know of that needs prayer, but specifically, name them and their needs.*
>
> *Years ago, I heard a CEO comment on what surprised her most about her job. She said it was when she gave her employees their reviews, she would ask them what they wanted for a raise, and 9 out of 10 times they would ask for less than she was willing to give them! Wow, if they had only known. So, in life, I say, pray and ask big. Think about it... when we find out someone is sick what do we typically pray for? So often we pray for the person to have the strength to endure the illness, for patience, for their family.*

We don't ask for healing — we don't go for the miracle! The general thinking is if the person is sick then God's will must be for that person to be ill, and we certainly don't want to go against God's will. But just as Scripture says, we are called to ASK. To the person who says, "What if it's not God's will to heal the person?" I say, "What if it is? What if God is just waiting for someone to ask Him?" God is a gentleman. So, when people ask me to pray for them, and they are sick, I always ask for complete healing. If it's a situation where the doctors say the person can't be healed, I think, ok, it's going to be easier for God to get the glory on this one when the person is healed. There was a lady in my Bible study group whose son's eardrum shattered and the doctor said he'll never hear out of that ear again. But we didn't stop praying for him after that diagnosis. And you know what, his hearing has slightly started to return, praise be to God, and we are continuing to pray for complete restoration of that ear!

My Bible lists Jesus' miracles in chronological order — of the 35 miracles, 27 were regarding HEALING. When Jesus was here on Earth people regularly came to Him for healing and He never once turned anyone away. Think about that — He healed everyone who asked. And I believe He will do the same for us today. In Pope Benedict's new book Jesus of Nazareth, *he says of Jesus, "He does not come bearing the sword of the revolutionary. He comes with the gift of healing. Healing our bodies, souls, spirits, our marriages, families, friendships, neighbors, countries, and yes, our world."*

I love the way Pam encourages us to go for it. Go for the miracle. God can handle it. Steer away from general prayers; the HOLY SPIRIT will help you. They lack faith and therefore are generally ineffective. Be specific, go for it. It is hard, but be daring. It is much easier to ask for strength or for help rather than for something specific (especially out loud). We worry and think, "What if it doesn't happen?" We are afraid of failure or making God look bad. Let God worry about God. He can handle Himself. It's His name at stake, not yours.

Most of the time, we don't ask for specific things because we lack faith. We think, "God may not want that for me," or "God has better things to do than to worry about my daughter's acne or my headache." I remember a man named John who came by one evening during Bible study needing prayer, and I offered to pray with him. He said, "I was just diagnosed with stage 4 cancer." I got help from my friends, and we all held hands and began to pray.

All of a sudden I felt the Holy Spirit urging me, and I said, "John, did you know that in all the gospels, throughout the gospels, no one ever asked Jesus to give them strength? NEVER! They always asked for the healing. Jesus would say, "What do you want?" and their responses would be, "Lord, heal me," or "Heal my daughter." They would say "I want to see," or "I want to walk.""

No one ever said to Jesus, "Leave me the way I am, just give me the strength to get through it." But that is how we pray. We are so afraid God won't do it that we don't even want to ask. He said to me, "Yes, Yes, that is all I want. I just want the strength to get through this." I realized that he did not hear what I was saying. Before I could think, before I could evaluate the words coming into my head, I blurted out, "Well, I say stage 4 to stage zero in the name of Jesus." I didn't hear from him until someone from church came to me and asked me if I had heard about John. He received good news from the doctor, "stage one", and he was telling everyone that God heard our prayer. When I ran into John on Easter Sunday, we hugged and cried and praised God together.

So many people are afraid to ask for healing for this reason. "What if God doesn't? If God doesn't heal, I will be left with nothing. If God doesn't heal and I stepped out and asked, what will people think?" Many, many choose not to ask so as not to be disappointed or risk looking unfaithful.

God healed me of allergies.

When I was pregnant with my youngest child 21 years ago. I had terrible allergies and did not want to take allergy medicine while pregnant. I was leading a prayer group at the time, and we ended every meeting with a squeeze prayer. Each of us would say a prayer and then squeeze the hand of the person next to us in the circle so they can ask and so on. When it was my turn to pray, I asked God to take away my allergies in the name of Jesus. I will never forget how many laughed at my prayer as if it was too hard for God. I was serious.

That fall while pregnant with David, I never sneezed. I did not receive one allergy symptom that year. God took those allergies away from me so completely and utterly that when they tried to come back on me the following year, I resisted and said, "NO WAY! I WAS HEALED! By His stripes, I WAS HEALED." I stood my ground and beat those symptoms down every time they rose up to retake their place attacking me. I refused them entrance.

God taught me how to fight. Every time a symptom showed its ugly face I began praying in tongues and declaring my freedom in the mighty name of Jesus, sometimes out loud.

Every day the symptoms would flee. It was miraculous. Even to this day, I can't sneeze without commanding my body into obedience to Jesus.

One day I remember growing weary of the battle. I said, "I am so tired..." and I heard God whisper to me, "Really? You are tired of praying for 10 minutes?" At that moment my daughter sneezed and I said, "No, Lord, I am not tired, forgive me." Ten minutes of prayer was all it took each day. Sometimes it took 2 or 3 ten-minute periods, if the devil was particularly relentless and testing my resolve. He will test your resolve.

Today I am completely allergy free and so is my family.

> **Matthew 6:30-33** *"O you of little faith? So do not worry and say, 'What are we to eat?' or 'What are we to drink?' or 'What are we to wear?' All these things the pagans seek. Your heavenly Father knows that you need them all. But seek first the kingdom of God and His righteousness, and all these things will be given you besides."*

WHY ARE SO MANY BELIEVERS STILL SICK?

If God said ask and you will receive, why do we not receive? There are many obstacles to healing: unforgiveness, complaining, doubt...

When we are sick, we tend to complain and moan. We can't seem to get our eyes off of the pain or sickness. We talk as if we have not asked God to heal us. We speak as though we don't believe God has heard our prayer, let alone that He is acting on it. If we truly believe God hears our prayers and is doing something about it, then we should not talk as if we are still sick and as if we are never going to be healed.

Complaining gets us nowhere but sick. Complaining is a lack of faith. Imagine how God must feel when we ask for healing and then begin to panic and worry.

Another trap that keeps us sick is sympathy. We want others to feel sorry for us when we are sick, but this just keeps us sick. If you are honest with yourself and recognize that you are enjoying or flirting with sympathy, you will be better equipped to fight against it. I want you to recognize when it's happening and do something about it. When you want sympathy, you don't want to be well. You can't have both sympathy and healing. Do you want to be pitiful or powerful?

If you use sickness as an excuse to get out of something, you may open the door to illness. Never use a headache as an excuse to get out of a meeting, a chore, or something you don't want to do. If you do, you may open the door to illness. You have made sickness an ally, a friend. Don't ever lie and say you are too sick to do something.

The most important obstacle to healing is a lack of forgiveness. Jesus said, "When you stand to pray, forgive anyone against whom you have a grievance, so that your heavenly Father may in turn forgive you your transgressions." (Mark 11:25)

Unforgiveness will not keep God from healing you but it may keep you from receiving it. Your heart will condemn you and it's hard to believe for healing when you are walking in hate and bitterness. Forgiveness is a decision. Just make it. Make it for God's sake and yours if not for the person you need to forgive.

Jesus came bearing gifts of healing and deliverance, and He gave them away freely and generously. He gave then, and He is still giving now. He does not have favorites. He does not love the leper in Matthew Chapter 8 more than you. He doesn't love the blind man, the lame, the beggar, the paralytic, the demoniac, the Centurion's servant, the daughter of the Canaanite woman, the woman with the issue of blood, or the countless others in the gospels more than you. The Bible says that our God is the God that heals. Healing is a gift that needs to be received.

Mark 9:23 Jesus said, *"EVERYTHING IS possible for him who believes."*

Mark 10:27 Jesus said, *"ALL THINGS are possible for God."*

Download my list of Healing Scriptures and read them every day. https://www.spiritfilledcatholic.com/healing/

You may not have enough faith, but the good news is you can have enough faith. Faith comes from God and it is a free gift. Faith comes as you read God's word or listen to it. I find after just a few minutes of reading God's Word I am filled with faith. Try it. Don't give up too quickly. Call on the Holy Spirit to give you understanding of God's words. Get ready to go places in the Spirit you have never been before and to keep on going. Make the word of God your daily manna.

The very first scripture is Proverbs 4:20-22, which says,

"My son, to my words be attentive, to my sayings incline your ear;Let them not slip from your sight, keep them within your heart; For they are life to those who find them, bringing health to one's whole being."

If the word of God brings health to one's whole being, isn't it worth reading when you are sick? If you are fearful and worried, read Psalm 91. If you are depressed and having nightmares, read Psalm 91 out loud before you go to bed. This Psalm is full of promises to you.

Be a warrior today and fight. Take God's word and stand on it and believe it's for you. The Word of God is sharper than any double-edged sword (Hebrews 4:12). The Word of God is an offensive weapon against the enemy (Ephesians 6:17). I have for you below an example of how to take the Word of God and pray it. Make it a personal prayer to God.

First read the scripture passage, then pray it or personalize it.

PSALM 91

1 Those who live in the shelter of the Most High will find rest in the shadow of the Almighty. 2 This I declare about the Lord: He alone is my refuge, my place of safety; He is my God, and I trust Him. 3 For He will rescue you from every trap and protect you from deadly disease.
4 He will cover you with His feathers. He will shelter you with His wings. His faithful promises are your armor and protection.

5 Do not be afraid of the terrors of the night, nor the arrow that flies in the day. 6 Do not dread the disease that stalks in darkness, nor the disaster that strikes at midday. 7 Though a

thousand fall at your side, though ten thousand are dying around you, these evils will not touch you.
8 Just open your eyes, and see how the wicked are punished.

9 If you make the Lord your refuge, if you make the Most High your shelter, 10 no evil will conquer you; no plague will come near your home. 11 For He will order His angels to protect you wherever you go. 12 They will hold you up with their hands so you won't even hurt your foot on a stone. 13 You will trample upon lions and cobras; you will crush fierce lions and serpents under your feet! 14 The Lord says, "I will rescue those who love Me. I will protect those who trust in My name. 15 When they call on Me, I will answer; I will be with them in trouble. I will rescue and honor them. 16 I will reward them with a long life and give them my salvation."

Praying Psalm 91 (Personalizing it)

I live in the shelter of the Most High. I rest in His shadow. My Lord is my refuge, my place of safety. He is my God and I trust Him. He rescues me (*put name of loved one here*) from every trap and protects me (*loved one*) from deadly diseases. He covers me with His feathers and shelters me with His wings. He protects me with His promises and is faithful regarding them.

I am not afraid of the terror of the night nor the arrow that flies by day. I am not afraid of disease or cancer.I am not afraid of any disaster. Nothing will harm me. Though many are dying around me from the same disease it will not touch me!

The Lord is my refuge. He is my shelter.
No evil will conquer me. No plague will come near my
home His angels protect me wherever I go. They will hold
me up and keep me protected. I will rise up and trample on
lions and cobras, depression and disease, cancer! They are
under my feet. I am loved and rescued by God because He
loves me, and I love Him.I trust in his name. I call upon him
and He answers me. He is with me in trouble. He has
rescued me and honors me and is rewarding me and
(LOVED ONE) with long life and salvation.

14

DEVIL

A few facts you may want to know about the devil.

1. The devil comes to kill, steal and destroy (John 10:10).
2. The devil is a liar, schemer, deceiver, and accuser.
3. The devil is defeated.

He wants to kill you, steal your faith and hope, and destroy your testimony with lies, schemes, and deception using shame and guilt to lure and trap you. Jesus gave us authority over all the power of the enemy (Luke 10:19). Let's use it.

The devil is the enemy of God. He wants us to grow in his image. Whose image are you becoming? Who do you represent? Who do you look or act like? The devil wants to tell us who we are and define us. He wants us hateful, spiteful, resentful, unforgiving, and bitter, just like he is. The Devil wants you on your knees before him cowering, fearful and anxious. He wants you in a fetal position afraid of the past, present, and the future. He wants you faithless. He wants us feeling rejected and an outcast, and he does it with thoughts and triggers. We were not made in his image; we were made in the image of our maker. The devil hates that about us and will steal it from us if we let him.

The enemy comes at us every day. He is relentless and ruthless. You have to be ready, alert, and armed. You are armed and dangerous; you just don't know it. You have been armed and well supplied with everything you need to, not only battle, but to win. The devil knows this, but you and I forget. We live in this world 24 hours a day, 7 days a week and we give God just one or two hours of our attention each week. It is not enough to drown out the world and all the lies of the enemy; it's not enough to combat the onslaught delivered to our mind and soul each week through television, the Internet, friends, music, movies, etc.

Because of Jesus, the devil has no power or authority over you. The devil thought he won when he convinced Judas to betray Jesus. When Jesus died, the devil believed he won. But he certainly wasn't prepared for what came next. Jesus conquered death! He destroyed death and fear and depression and ALL THE WORKS OF THE ENEMY. Jesus conquered death and proved it by rising from the dead!

> **Colossians 2:14-15** *He canceled the record of the charges against us and took it away by nailing it to the cross. In this way, He disarmed the spiritual rulers and authorities. He shamed them publicly by His victory over them on the cross."*

The only thing the devil has to use against us has been taken away by Jesus at the cross - OUR SINS - and therefore all guilt and shame. The devil can no longer accuse us if we know we are forgiven. Jesus said whom the Son sets free is free indeed. We just have to understand it and believe it. When we do, the devil is powerless against us. How can he accuse someone who knows he has been exonerated?

Did you know that the devil is no competition for God? There is no power struggle going on between good and evil. Good destroyed evil at the cross where Jesus crushed death and sin and all the power of hell. God wins every time. Which means you win every time. You may lose a battle here and there, but you win the war. You win because Jesus already fought it and won. He rose from the dead and because you are with Him and in Him, you too rose from the dead to new life in Him.

God exalted Jesus to the highest place and gave Him authority over all. He gave Jesus the name that is highly exalted over every other name. At the name of Jesus, every knee must bend (Philippians 2:10). This is the same name He gave us. Jesus said in Mark 16:17 "These signs will accompany those who believe: in My name you will drive out demons." We have authority over demons because Jesus gave it to us.

It's as simple as that yet so hard to believe.

Against a child of God, the devil is powerless, though he won't quit trying to seduce you and accuse you and lure you. He will continue to harass you until it quits working on you. As long as you believe his lies, he will keep trying. He will scare you and lie to you and try to get you to do things his way, but he cannot succeed unless you let him and actually follow him. He is relentless and persuasive, but powerless

The only power he has is the power we give him. The devil will try to intimidate you, but remind him that he was conquered and disarmed (see Colossians above). His power over us was dismantled; deactivated. His accusations against us were nullified at the cross. You have to recognize him and his tactics, so you don't follow him down into the pit.

God has equipped us with powerful tools and weapons. We have His Word and His Name, which gives us the authority we need to trample and tread and annihilate the enemy that has already been overpowered and destroyed.

Mark 16:17 *"In my name you will cast out demons."*

Luke 10:19 *"Behold, I have given you authority to tread on serpents and scorpions, and over all the power of the enemy, and nothing will injure you."*

YOU HAVE POWER over ALL the power of evil, God says. You should never be afraid of anything the devil throws your way because the Greater One lives in you. Don't let images from the television or a movie or stories you heard growing up influence you. Get those thoughts and pictures out of your head. You are not ruled by demons, they are afraid of you, so much so that they will do anything to keep you from learning who you really are. You are royalty, heirs to the Kingdom of God, the child of God himself. Once you realize who you are and the power you have to cast them away, they will run from you.

As long as we don't know that, the enemy will have his way with us and keep spoon-feeding us anxiety, fear, hate, offense, pride, jealousy, sickness, and whatever else we will accept and believe is ours to keep and endure.

Recognizing him is half the battle. When I recognize it's the devil wreaking havoc in my life or trying to get me to pout and be offended, I WANT to resist. I want to rebuke him, refuse, reject, and renounce him and his kingdom. I don't want to do his will.

Jesus did not leave us defenseless or powerless, but He left us strong and powerful. The Spirit of God lives in us, and this power is the same power that raised Jesus from the dead.

> **Ephesians 1:19-20** *"I also pray that you will understand the incredible greatness of God's power for us who believe Him. This is the same mighty power that raised Christ from the dead and seated Him in the place of honor at God's right hand in the heavenly realms."*

It's very important to know who you are in Christ and what is yours. When we know who we are and what is ours, we can fight the devil and all his thoughts from a position of authority and confidence. We won't just give in or run in fear or cower and just accept things as they are. We will be willing to take back what the enemy stole from us, such as our peace and kindness, gentleness... We become strong in the Lord and in His mighty power.

> **Ephesians 6:10-13** *"Finally, draw your strength from the Lord and from His mighty power. Put on the armor of God so that you may be able to stand firm against the tactics of the devil. For our struggle is not with flesh and blood but with the principalities, with the powers, with the world rulers of this present darkness, with the evil spirits in the heavens. Therefore, put on the armor of God, that you may be able to resist on the evil day and, having done everything, to hold your ground."*

LET'S PRACTICE

Only God can read your thoughts. The devil can send thoughts your way, but he can't understand what you're thinking. He is not GOD. He is not omnipresent or omnipotent. We give him too much power.

Keep your mouth shut, and he won't know the thoughts of fear and terror and worry he sends are effective. Don't talk about how afraid you are.

Declare this out loud, so the devil can hear you.

> *"I am a child of the most High God. Jesus is my Lord and savior. He is my healer and my deliverer. I can do all things through Christ who paid for all my sins on the cross. He died for me so I can live and He took with Him all my sicknesses and diseases as well. Now I can declare in faith that I am well and these symptoms are lies. By His Stripes, I am well."*

When those pesky symptoms rise, beat them down.

> *"I resist you, nausea, in the name of Jesus. I am well. I rebuke you and command you off of me. The blood of the Lamb has washed me, and I am hidden in Him, cleansed and forgiven. I belong to Jesus, and I trust Him with my life. I command my body into obedience to Jesus Christ. My mind, my thoughts, my organs, bones, and systems."*

We are either victorious or not. We are either "In Christ" or not. Victory is ours, or it isn't. You and I have to decide that the Word of God is true and stand on it. When the devil throws sickness and symptoms on you, fight back, don't just roll over and play dead. Speak God's Word out loud. Reject those symptoms. You can, and you must. Reject that runny and itchy nose. Reject that nausea, or that diagnosis that says it's hopeless. You have the Greater One living inside of you. There is hope. Don't worry or think about all those who died sick. Believe more in God's Word than anyone else's circumstances. Today is a new day for you, a day to pick up God's Word and believe.

Here is a handy warfare CARD! When in doubt come in the name of Jesus against the spirit of infirmity. When Jesus saw the woman bent over in Luke Chapter 13, He set her free of her infirmity.

- **RECOGNIZE** Recognize the deceiver and know when you are being toyed with.
- **RESIST** The Bible says to submit to God, resist the devil, and he will flee from you. "Jesus You are my Lord and Savior; I submit to you."
- **REFUSE** Refuse to listen or give the devil your time or attention.
- **REJECT** Refuse his thoughts and lies and command your thoughts into obedience to Christ. "I command..."
- **RENOUNCE** Renounce all ties and close any doors you have opened to the devil. "I renounce the spirit of ____ and your hold on me is broken."
- **REBUKE** "_____, I command you , in the name of Jesus, to leave me."

For copies of this card to download or order go to https://www.spiritfilledcatholic.com/downloads

RE	RECOGNIZE	*Recognize the deceiver and know when you are being toyed with.*
RE	RESIST	*The Bible says to submit yourself to God, resist the devil and he will flee from you. "Jesus, you are my Lord and Savior, I submit to you.*
RE	REFUSE	*Refuse to listen or give the voices, thoughts, or symptoms your time or attention.*
RE	REJECT	*Reject his thoughts and lies and command your thoughts into obedience to Jesus. "I command my thoughts ... "*
RE	RENOUNCE	*Renounce all ties and close any doors you have opened to the devil. "I renounce (sin, occult, words I have spoken or others have spoken). Your hold on me is broken.*
RE	REBUKE	*Command the spirit to leave you. "Spirit of infirmity, _____, I command you, in the name of Jesus to leave me."*

15

SUICIDE

A note from my 21 year old friend Mackenzie who attempted suicide when she was 13 years old.

"As I look back I think about what I would have missed if I had waited a little longer before telling my mother.

By the grace of God I told my mom, 5 hours after taking a bottle of pills. For some reason I thought surely 5 hours was long enough enough to get the job done. I thought I had passed the point of no return. I wanted to tell my mom because I thought she would be comforted knowing that she tried her best to save me.

The first night is some what of a blur. I just remember them having to clean my liver out for about 4-5 days with powerful IV medication. But to be honest I don't remember much.

I would have missed so much if I had been successful.

The problem with depression is that you get so sad that you see no hope, no future and no peace.

I would have missed seeing the beauty of the world!

I would have missed having the most successful academic year of my life! I would have missed meeting my best friends Hannah and Jessica. I would have missed out on life if I had been successful.

The devil tries to keep us depressed by putting blinders on our eyes and fog in our brains. He tries to prevent us from seeing a future. He tries to keep a grasp on our minds and feeds us lies that things will never get better. The devil likes to tell you that "so and so" won't miss you. He may even tell you that God wants you dead too. The devil likes to whisper lies that life will be better if we were dead. But it would not be better because we would be dead. We would have missed out on the life that God had planned for us.

I would have missed having a college experience. I would have missed out on joining a dating website my freshmen year of college. I would have missed out on swimming in the beautiful seas of Greece. I would have missed out on finally having normal life (lol my life ain't an ounce normal).

I write this to share that things do get better. But I know when you are so deep down in depression and the devil lies to you saying you should end your life, please don't. People always told me just wait, soon it will get better. But we can not see the "it will get better." I only write this to share... take it from the girl who tried so desperately to end her own life.

Depression is a liar!

But with the Grace of God I pray that you and all who are depressed may see the world with a clear lens and that God may cleanse your heart, eyes and mind from depression, suicidal thoughts, and lies from the devil. I pray that you, like me, see and feel the truth of God.

I truly believe that there is nothing we can say to prevent someone who is contemplating suicide. We can try our best to protect them and keep them safe, but if the blinders, fogged vision, and lies from the devil are strong and fierce, the only thing we can do is pray. And by ONLY, I mean you NEED to pray. Lay hands on the person's head and pray!

A group of women came to my house and prayed in my bedroom! My mom painted a huge wall with bible verses in my room! Pray that the Lord, our God, cleanses their mind from depression! Pray that they get the right medication. Pray that they receive the right counseling! Pray, pray, pray! Pray with faith that God will work in their mind and wake them up from depression.

If you know someone who was successful in their attempt, know that they could not see a way out of their hurt. Please know in your heart that there wasn't anything more you could have done. Please stop thinking "if only I did ___." Suicide is a tool the devil uses. You didn't know.

Your loved one did not mean to hurt you. They truly thought it was best. They could not see an alternative to their pain. Please know that they were hurting and could not see any way out. Even if they were in the hospital or sleeping next to you, a person who is that depressed may attempt suicide no matter what you do to try to protect them. So please stop thinking "if only I did ___."

If you are contemplating ending your own life please, I beg you, ask for help! Go to the hospital! I beg you! Your feelings and thoughts are real right now (to you), but things will get better! I know, I know you can not see it now but please, please hold on. Fall to your knees in prayer and reach out to someone. Call, check your self into a hospital.

I would have missed out on these 7-8 years of life. I would have missed out on loving life. I would have missed out on falling completely and utterly in Love with the Holy Spirit. I would have missed out on so much if I had been successful.

Mackenzie Fanatico

NATIONAL SUICIDE PREVENTION HOTLINE 1-800-273-8255

A real live person will answer the phone, stay on the line. You will talk with someone who wants to help you or who is there just to talk. You matter to me. You matter to God. It may be dark and lonely, and you may hear voices, but this is not your future.

16

BE LIKE DAVID AND TAKE DOWN GOLIATH

Do You Have a Goliath That Needs to Be Destroyed?

God Doesn't Play Around with Evil. He Took Care of It. The story of David and Goliath is found in 1 Samuel, Chapter 17.

This passage has the battle plan for you when you are under attack and facing something that is bigger and stronger than you. Goliath was huge and a force no one wanted to face. Just hearing his voice brought terror and dismay to the whole army of Israel. Is something terrorizing you? Today is the day we turn the tables on that which has us on the run and in fear for our lives. Today we recognize the Greater One living in us.

The Philistines gathered their forces for war against the Israelites. Each army occupied a hill with the valley in between them. Every day for 40 days, the Philistines sent Goliath out to taunt the Israelites. He would shout at them and say, "Send someone to fight me. If I win, you and your armies will serve us. If you win, we will be your servants."

Goliath said, "This day I defy the ranks of Israel! Give me a man and let us fight each other." The whole Israelite army was afraid of Goliath, and no one thought they could defeat him. David was a shepherd boy and was sent to the front lines to bring food to his brothers and their commanders. When he arrived, he saw Goliath, the Philistine champion, step out from the battle line shouting his "usual defiance."

David watched as the army of Israel ran from him in great fear. All the Israelites were afraid of Goliath. They had no confidence. They forgot who was on their side. They kept their eyes on Goliath. They kept their eyes on the problem in front of them. It made them nervous and sick, and they grew defeated and helpless.

When David showed up on the scene, he couldn't believe what he saw. He saw the whole Israelite army afraid of Goliath. The Bible describes the scene, "They all fled from Goliath in great fear." David, a youth, said, "What? You are afraid of him, an uncircumcised man who defies the God of Israel?"

David continued, "Let me at him. I have taken care of the lion and the bear. God has protected me then, and He will protect me from this." David was amazed that the Israelite troops had forgotten God. David was astonished that they did not recognize Goliath as an enemy of God.

David said to Saul, the king of Israel. "Do not be afraid, I will go fight this Philistine." "But you are just a boy," the king said. "I used to take care of my father's sheep," David told him, "and when a bear or lion would come and take one, I would run after it and rescue it from his mouth. If he turned on me, I seized him by the hair of his jaw and struck him down and killed him. This Philistine will be like one of them for he has dared to insult the armies of the living God."

We need to be like David, who recognized Goliath as defeated, merely a bear or lion that needed to be killed. Just like the bears and lions didn't stand a chance against David, neither would this Goliath. David was the only one who knew it, though. The entire army was afraid of Goliath. Goliath posed no threat to David because David knew Goliath was uncircumcised and defying the Great I Am. He knew Goliath could be beaten because Goliath was fighting God himself by coming against the people of God.

Goliath saw David approach him and began to curse him. He tried to terrorize him, but David was unmoved. Goliath said to David, "Come here, and I will give your flesh to the birds of the air and the beasts of the field!"

David, however, did not flinch. The words that struck terror in the whole army did nothing to David. David had confidence in God. David knew who His God was; he knew what His God was capable of, and he had no doubt that God would go before him. David knew that God would show up. He was the only one who knew. No one else had faith that God was on their side.

They didn't know their Father was the God of the universe, or they sure didn't act like it. David knew just how big God was and just how small Goliath was. The Israelites saw Goliath as huge and themselves as small and insignificant against such an enemy. They saw the situation as impossible, but David had a different perspective, one that included GOD. David knew he was God's anointed one. He knew he was called and chosen.

DO YOU?

Do you let Goliath win, beat you down and terrorize you? Do you remember to whom you belong? Jesus made you God's child. You are blessed because you are His. You are empowered because you are His.

> **John 1:12** *"But to those who did accept him he gave power to become children of God."*

This force coming against you in the form of sickness or depression, fear or anxiety, has no chance because when it comes against you, it is coming against God himself. Whoever comes against you, the King's child, comes against the very King Himself. You are a Christian. Being a Christian is not just a matter of getting something or going somewhere, it's a matter of being someone — someone special.

David's mountain started talking to him. GOLIATH began to chide David.

> **1 Samuel 17:42–44** *"He looked David over and saw that he was little more than a boy, glowing with health and handsome, and he despised him. He said to David, 'Am I a dog, that you come at me with sticks ?' And the Philistine cursed David by his gods. 'Come here ,' he said, 'and I'll give your flesh to the birds and the wild animals!'"*

It's a good thing David did not listen. Don't listen to that mountain speaking to you when you can't fall asleep at night. Know where to turn your ear. David knew not to let Goliath intimidate him.

If you listen and pay heed to Goliath or your mountains, they will talk to you. Your mountains will tell you lies all day and keep you up at night. Have you ever been up all night worrying? This is your mountain talking back to you. Do you find yourself angry, unable to control yourself? It's time to take control and start speaking to your mountains and telling them where to go and who is in charge.

David didn't pay attention to Goliath. Instead, he answered him. Listen carefully to David's reply. It must be your reply as well to temptation and sickness.

> 1 Samuel 17:45-49 *"David said to the Philistine, "You come against me with sword and spear and javelin, but I come against you in the name of the LORD Almighty, the God of the armies of Israel, whom you have defied. This day the LORD will deliver you into my hands, and I'll strike you down and cut off your head. This very day I will give the carcasses of the Philistine army to the birds and the wild animals, and the whole world will know that there is a God in Israel. All those gathered here will know that it is not by sword or spear that the LORD saves; for the battle is the LORD's, and he will give all of you into our hands." As the Philistine moved closer to attack him, David ran quickly toward the battle line to meet him. Reaching into his bag and taking out a stone, he slung it and struck the Philistine on the forehead. The stone sank into his forehead, and he fell face down on the ground."*

So here is the Word of God to use when you come up against your opponent, or your personal mountain, such as depression. Let's paraphrase what David said to fight the stronghold of depression.

I come against you, depression, in the name of the Lord Almighty, and in the name of Jesus whom you have defied. This day the Lord will deliver you, depression, into my hands, and I will strike you down, depression, and cut off your head. This very day I will give the carcass of depression to the birds and the wild animals and the whole world will know that there is a God.

Fill in the above lines with debt, sickness, or whatever your stronghold is. "**I COME AGAINST YOU spirit of infirmity...**" If you still do not think you are allowed to speak and command, listen again to what Jesus says in the Gospel of Luke.

Luke 10:17–19 *"The seventy-two returned with joy and said, "Lord, even the demons submit to us in your name.'" He replied, "I saw Satan fall like lightning from heaven. I have given you authority to trample on snakes and scorpions and to overcome all the power of the enemy; nothing will harm you.'"*

God wants you bringing down Goliath. Right now.

David was anointed, and so are you. The same Holy Spirit that empowered David lives on the inside of you. You too can speak like David. Don't let these symptoms rule you or define you. You have the same power David did. You can crush the head of the serpent/the devil/sickness/depression. You have the power. You just don't know you do. God has given you power over all the power of the enemy, Jesus said in Luke 10:19. You have power over shyness, fear, worry, every diagnosis, sickness, depression, and all thoughts that torment you.

David knew His God was bigger than his mountain. David knew God was on his side. You too have to believe without a doubt that God is for you and not against you. Believe God is on your side. He is. If you are in Christ, God is on your side. Don't doubt it, ever.

SPEAK...

David triumphed because losing was not an option. Don't quit. Speak until it's done.

David triumphed over Goliath and so will you. Be bold. It's worth it. David rescued a whole nation that day because he simply did not doubt and was willing to take on Goliath when no one else would. Are you willing to save your family? Are you willing to be so bold for the sake of those who come after you? Are you sowing seeds of fear and worry or seeds of victory? Today is the day you stand up and fight until you win. Do not back down. God will not let you down. You cannot have too much faith in God.

God will never fail you. He will never let you down and He will never disappoint you.The Bible says so in Deuteronomy 31:8 and Hebrews 13:5-6 and throughout the pages of the Bible. If God has failed you in the past, reconsider who you were leaning on and counting on. God won't let you down, You may let you down, the government may let your down, the doctors and medicines may let you down, but God will never let you down. Don't quit believing too soon.

The Israelite army forgot who was on their side; they kept their eyes on Goliath. They kept their eyes on the problem in front of them. It made them nervous and sick, and they grew defeated and helpless. Keep your eyes on God as David did. Evil is always looming. Worry and fear are always crouching at the door waiting for you to open it just a crack. As soon as you feel the sickness, or your thoughts change to fearful thoughts, shut the door. Slam it! Turn to God immediately. The devil is always searching for a crack in your armor. Remain looking at Jesus. Turn now. Fix your eyes on Jesus and say with confidence and hope, "I TRUST YOU, Jesus."

David knew God because he had a relationship with God. He knew God well and knew God would fight for him just like He always had in the past. If only we had such faith. If only we had such a relationship with God. If only we trusted. But many times, our faith is in what we see, hear, and smell, just the like the army of Israel. Trust in the God you cannot see. Trust in the one who died for you. He died for you so you would know how much He loves you. He died for you so you would know He will be there for you in your time of need.

> 1 John 4:4 *"You belong to God, children, and you have conquered them, for the one who is in you is greater than the one who is in the world."*

17

SACRAMENT OF RECONCILIATION

James 5:16 "Therefore, confess your sins to
one another and pray for one another,
that you may be healed."

The Sacrament of Reconciliation is a gift and offers us the privilege of coming before God and man to confess our sins, knowing fully that He already forgave us at the cross, knowing fully that we are forgiven. What a gift. It isn't a law or an obligation; it is a "Get To." We simply get to go to confession. What an opportunity the Church offers us. God isn't waiting to forgive; He already made the decision to forgive us 2000 years ago. He doesn't say YES and/or NO! He simply says yes when we come to Him. He knows our heart and to whom we belong.

So, confess your sins to one another and be free and healed. If there is a sin that is bothering you, which is causing you stress and agitation, confess it to someone you trust. If you are Catholic, I recommend the Sacrament of Reconciliation. You will leave light and free from guilt because the devil will no longer be able to accuse you. Once it's confessed, his hold over you is broken. He can't accuse you of a sin you know you confessed. All you have to do is remember, Jesus has it.

Confession helps us to remember it is forgiven. When the Devil accuses you, you have the memory of confessing it and the assurance it has no more power over you. Sometimes we just need to hear those words

"You are forgiven."

We know when we sin. Our hearts condemn us. We have been made pure through Christ so when we sin, we know it, we feel it. Confess it and get over it. Confession helps us get past it. We stop letting it condemn us. Confession puts an end to condemnation from that voice within. We know when we sin, we know when we fail and we know we will again, but we also know Jesus took our sins. We are forgiven.

I will not deny the cross by believing I am still condemned. Jesus died for me to set me free. I have to believe it. I believe He did it for me. My sins are not too big for Him. Nothing is greater than the cross. No sin is greater than Jesus' death. If I don't believe I am forgiven then I deny the power of the cross; the suffering Jesus bore for me. If, however, I believe that I am forgiven, I am accepting the power of the cross.

Galatians 2:21 *"I do not nullify the grace of God; for if justification comes through the law, then Christ died for nothing."*

Isaiah 53: 4-6 " *Yet it was our pain that he bore, our sufferings he endured. We thought of him as stricken, struck down by God and afflicted, but he was pierced for our sins, crushed for our*

iniquity. He bore the punishment that makes us whole, by his wounds we were healed. We had all gone astray like sheep, all following our own way; but the Lord laid upon him the guilt of us all.

Isaiah 1:18 " *Come now, let us set things right, says the Lord: Though your sins be like scarlet, they may become white as snow; though they be red like crimson, they may become white as wool.*"

We need to know we can go to the Father, sinful or not. He wants us just the way we are, sin and all. He is our savior, deliverer, redeemer, all-powerful one, not us. We cannot save ourselves. We cannot redeem ourselves. We can do nothing without Him. He is the one that cleanses us from all our sins. He makes us holy.

18

BATTLE PLAN: HOW TO FIGHT

You and I are in a spiritual battle and Jesus left us with everything we need to live in peace, prosperity and victory. Jesus left us with His Name, His Word, the Holy Spirit, and the Church. We have everything we need to battle and win. We have already won. The battles we fight are from a position of victory because we are His. If only we could remember we are on the winning side, we would be confident and always at peace.

> 2 Corinthians 10: 3–5 *"For though we live in the world, we do not wage war as the world does. The weapons we fight with are not the weapons of the world. On the contrary, they have divine power to demolish strongholds. We demolish arguments and every pretension that sets itself up against the knowledge of God, and we take captive every thought to make it obedient to Christ."*

The weapons at our disposal are spiritual, and they are powerful because, when we use them, we have all the power of heaven behind us. Just like David when he went up against Goliath. You too have spiritual forces behind you. You, like David, are armed. Listen to what the Bible says about the battle.

> **2 Chronicles 20:15** *"The Lord says to you: Do not fear or be dismayed at the sight of this vast multitude, for the battle is not yours but God's."*

> **2 Chronicles 20:17** *"You will not have to fight in this encounter. Take your places, stand firm, and see the salvation of the Lord; He will be with you, Judah and Jerusalem. Do not fear or be dismayed."*

> **1 Samuel 17:37** *"David continued: 'The same Lord who delivered me from the claws of the lion and the bear will deliver me from the hand of this Philistine.'"*

> **1 Samuel 17:47** *"All this multitude, too, shall learn that it is not by sword or spear that the Lord saves. For the battle belongs to the Lord, who shall deliver you into our hands."*

Are you ready for the battle plan? Here are your tools, and with them a strategy for overcoming anything and everything against you.

TOOLS FOR BATTLE

- THE HOLY SPIRIT
- PRAYER
- FAITH
- LOVE AND FORGIVENESS

- THE WORD OF God
- YOUR MOUTH
- JESUS
- PRAISE
- PR PR PR

19

TOOLS FOR BATTLE – THE HOLY SPIRIT

Before Jesus ascended into Heaven, He told His disciples to wait for the Holy Spirit. He told them not to leave Jerusalem, but to wait for the promise of the Father.

Jesus said, "You will receive POWER when the Holy Spirit comes upon you..."

> **Acts 1:4-8** "*While meeting with them, he enjoined them not to depart from Jerusalem, but to wait for "the promise of the Father about which you have heard Me speak; for John baptized with water, but in a few days you will be baptized with the Holy Spirit. When they had gathered together they asked him, 'Lord, are You at this time going to restore the kingdom to Israel?' He answered them, 'It is not for you to know the times or seasons that the Father has established by His own authority. But you will receive power when the holy Spirit comes upon you, and you will be my witnesses in Jerusalem, throughout Judea and Samaria, and to the ends of the earth.'*"

Jesus knew we couldn't do this life without help, which is why He said in...

John 16:7 *"I tell you the truth, it is better for you that I go. For if I do not go, the Advocate will not come to you. But if I go, I will send him to you."*

The Gift of God is His Holy Spirit. The Holy Spirit's main job is to reveal God to us. So many of us wonder if God is real? Are we following the one true God? Are we right? How do we know we have it right? Well, that is the job of the Holy Spirit. The Holy Spirit reveals Jesus to us. You supply the faith and God will confirm it through the Holy Spirit. You will have an encounter with God. God wants to reveal himself to you. Just wait and see.

Jesus told us that the Holy Spirit will teach us everything and lead us into all truth (John 14:26). The Holy Spirit will help you recognize a stronghold. The first step to victory and freedom is knowing what we are fighting and identifying it as evil.

Ask the Holy Spirit to show you what enslaves you. He will reveal strongholds in our lives if we want Him to. Ask the Holy Spirit. God's Word says He is our helper, "our ever-present help in time of need" (Psalm 46:1).

If you don't know whether or not you have a stronghold, ask the Holy Spirit. Do not try to investigate this on your own. He will point them out, so don't worry. The Holy Spirit is really good at it; it is His job. He will do it gently, correctly, and with love. He has ONLY your best interest at heart. The Holy Spirit won't point something out to you just to show off. He wants you delivered from its hold. If he reveals any area of bondage it is to deliver you from it.

Jesus told his disciples to wait in Jerusalem until they received power from above. Jesus is saying the same thing to you and me. Don't do anything until you receive power from the Holy Spirit; power to live for Him and die for Him. We received the Holy Spirit at Confirmation, but His power was not at our disposal because we were not walking with Jesus. The power of the Holy Spirit is ours now if we just ask. Renew your confirmation and receive power from the Holy Spirit.

> **Luke 11:13** *"If you then, who are wicked, know how to give good gifts to your children, how much more will the Father in heaven give the Holy Spirit to those who ask Him?"*

> **Acts 1:8** *"But you will receive power when the holy Spirit comes upon you, and you will be my witnesses in Jerusalem, throughout Judea and Samaria, and to the ends of the earth."*

The Holy Spirit comes to all who ask. If you want the Holy Spirit in your life, ask and then believe He is with *you.*

PRAYER: Father, I ask for an outpouring of the Holy Spirit and for His power and strength in my life. I ask for the power and strength to follow after Jesus and remain in Christ Jesus my Lord, with my eyes and heart fixed on him. I pray for the ability and desire to read and study your Word. I ask for wisdom and for the revelation knowledge of who You are, Lord. I want to know the hope You have for me for my family and all you have given to me. I want the power that is available to me to be the witness You have called me to be to my family, church, and the world around me. Fill me, Lord, to overflowing that I may walk boldly in your presence every day. Take me deeper and higher than I ever dreamed possible.

I need and desire you, Holy Spirit. I want to walk in Your ways, not the flesh. I want to be controlled by You, Holy Spirit, not my flesh. I want to receive all the gifts You choose to give me, so I can glorify You and walk in love, joy, peace, and all the fruit of the Spirit. Give me the courage to receive You and Your gifts. I choose You, Lord Jesus. Anoint me with Your power and the desire to be Your disciple.

Holy Spirit, enter my life so I may have...

- POWER to know and love Christ
- POWER to know the Word of God
- POWER to love others and extend mercy and grace
- POWER to witness
- POWER to act, to forgive
- POWER to live free from sin and worry and fear
- POWER to represent God
- POWER to show God's power through the gifts of the Holy Spirit
- POWER to crush evil spirits
- POWER to know God's will
- POWER to remain in God's will
- POWER to believe
- POWER to serve
- POWER to proclaim the good news

The Holy Spirit gives us gifts that we haven't even begun to use and develop. The gift of knowledge, wisdom, prophecy, discernment, tongues, interpretation of tongues, healing, faith, and signs and wonders. Tongues is one of my favorite weapons against the enemy, along with the Word of God. When I don't know how to pray, I pray in tongues. I let the Holy Spirit pray for me. He knows how to pray for me according to God's will and it's always perfect and powerful.

> **Romans 8:26** *"In the same way, the Spirit too comes to the aid of our weakness; for we do not know how to pray as we ought, but the Spirit itself intercedes with inexpressible groanings."*

> **Romans 8:9-11** *"But you are not in the flesh; on the contrary, you are in the spirit, if only the Spirit of God dwells in you. Whoever does not have the Spirit of Christ does not belong to Him. But if Christ is in you, although the body is dead because of sin, the spirit is alive because of righteousness. If the Spirit of the one who raised Jesus from the dead dwells in you, the one who raised Christ from the dead will give life to your mortal bodies also, through His Spirit that dwells in you."*

For more on the Holy Spirit get my Bible Study "The Holy Spirit, Lord and Giver of Life"

https://www.spiritfilledcatholic.com/books

20

TOOLS FOR BATTLE – PRAYER

God wants you. He wants an intimate relationship with you. He wants you to want Him and to want to spend time with Him. He wants to download to you everything. How much of God do you want? How much time do you have to give him? He wants to reveal Himself to you. Start where you are. If you give Him five minutes a day, stretch it to ten. You will not be disappointed. You can't out give God. He will not allow it.

Whatever you give Him in time or effort will accrue to your account. God always has to be the bigger giver. Just keep on giving and wait and see. Years later you will look back and not recognize yourself. God is doing a work in you. Be patient.

> **2 Corinthians 9:6** *"Whoever sows bountifully will reap bountifully."*

How do you pray? How you pray is important because most people pray incorrectly. I hear people all the time say, "I pray and pray and pray." Are you, too, praying and praying and praying and nothing is happening? What are we missing?

James 5:16....*The fervent prayer of a righteous person is very powerful.*"

Another version of the Bible says that the fervent prayer of the righteous is powerful and effective. There is a way to pray that is effective and powerful. Who doesn't want to pray effectively and with power? I am about to take you on the best ride of your life. Prayer is supposed to be exciting, and there is nothing like it. Prayer is not a chore but an experience. It is entering God's presence and experiencing a taste of heaven. Expect much from your prayer time. Prayer should be way more exciting than any movie, party or earthly experience.

Are you a righteous person? You are. You! You can't be righteous on your own but in Christ you are righteous. You have to know this and settle this once and for all in your heart. Once you know that your righteousness comes from Jesus, you will always approach God with confidence. This is why we always come to Him in the name of Jesus. We alone can never merit an audience with God. This is why God sent His Son. He did it for us. Our sins are no longer held against us because Jesus took them.

Prayer is communion or communicating with God. Prayer is a natural extension of being one with God and in a relationship with Him. Prayer is praising God, singing, hanging out with God, reading his word, telling him your problems, listening and waiting for Him, thanking him, and interceding for others.

The Catechism of the Catholic Church describes prayer as....

> **2564** *Christian prayer is a covenant relationship between God and man in Christ. It is the action of God and of man, springing forth from both the Holy Spirit and ourselves, wholly directed to the Father, in union with the human will of the Son of God made man.*

To Whom Do we Pray?

Don't be afraid to direct your prayer "wholly" to the Father. Prayer is first and foremost addressing the Father. Our Father wants to hear from us directly more than you know. Most of the time I pray directly to the Father like Jesus taught us and the church teaches us. I always pray in the name of Jesus. When his disciples asked him how to pray, He said to them, "When you pray, say, "Father, hallowed be Your name....'"

My favorite prayer is this: *"Father, Jesus said I could come to you for anything. He gave me full permission to approach you in his name. So I come to you, not for what I deserve, but for the mercy and grace Jesus won for me when He went to the cross."*

Prayer is asking. Never be afraid to ask. God loves it when we ask because asking suggests we need Him. It is an act of humility.

> **Matthew 7:7-8***"Ask, and it will be given to you; seek, and you will find; knock, and it will be opened to you. For everyone who asks receives, and he who seeks finds, and to him who knocks it will be opened."*

> **James 4:2** *"You do not have because you do not ask."*

God said we could come to him for anything so don't be shy. We are taught to pray CONFIDENTLY, FERVENTLY, IMMEDIATELY, CONTINUOUSLY and with FAITH

PRAY CONFIDENTLY

Our confidence comes from Jesus Christ, who gave His life so we could go directly to the Father boldly and with confidence. When Jesus died the veil was torn that separated God and man. When we go timidly and fearfully to God, begging and pleading, we act like we just don't know who we are and to whom we belong and that the way to the Father was opened. We act like we don't know what Jesus did for us. Jesus said we can ask the Father anything in His name. So act like you believe it.

> **Ephesians 3:12** *"In whom we boldness of speech and confidence of access through faith in him."*

Our confidence is not in ourselves or in our goodness or worthiness. If we approached the Father on our own, by our own merit, we would always find some reason to shy away. Jesus is our confidence.

> **Hebrews 4:16** *"Let us then approach the Throne of Grace with confidence so that we may receive mercy and find grace to help us in our time of need."*

Our confidence comes when we know we are His children and forgiven and made right before God. The son or daughter of the King can approach the throne whenever they like. We can go to God anytime and anywhere because we are special, thanks to Jesus, who makes us special.

Did you know that you are righteous? We are righteous, the Bible says, not because we are perfect but because we are in Christ. IN HIM, Christ, we are the righteousness of God.

> **2 Corinthians 5:21** *For our sake he made him to be sin who did not know sin, so that we might become the righteousness of God in him.*

Jesus made us righteous or "right" with God when He exchanged His righteousness for our sinfulness.

> **Romans 5:19** *"For just as through the disobedience of one person the many were made sinners, so through the obedience of one the many will be made righteous."*

He became sin for us so that our prayer is powerful and effective. Don't forget this! We forget this all the time. We lean on our own righteousness and always come up short. We trust God to answer our prayers based on our own righteousness, and therefore since we NEVER measure up, we never expect our prayers to be answered!!!

Righteousness is a gift. You don't have to win it or earn it or figure it out. Just know and believe that you are in Christ. Tell yourself "I am the righteousness of God in Christ Jesus." Read all of Romans Chapters 3, 4, and 5 to learn about what it means to be righteous because of Christ.

> **Mark 11:24** *"Therefore I tell you, whatever you ask for in prayer, believe that you have received it, and it will be yours."*

So go to the Father in confidence in the name of Jesus. That is why we have confidence. Our confidence is knowing Jesus is always accepted by the Father and through Him, so are we.

PRAY FERVENTLY

The Bible says that fervent prayer is powerful.

When was last time you prayed with passion or with intensity? I am not saying God is moved by how intense our prayer is, but sometimes we may need to pick it up a little.

How long should you pray? Pray until you have peace. When we pray for someone who is ill, we have to remember they are counting on us. Think of yourself as a lifeguard. The lifeguard doesn't quit swimming until they reach the person drowning.

PRAY CONTINUOUSLY

The Bible says to pray continuously.

> 1 Thessalonians 5:17 *"Pray without ceasing."*

When you don't know what to pray for or how to pray, pray in tongues. I pray in tongues daily, which allows me to pray even when I am working. When you pray "in tongues" you are allowing the Holy Spirit to pray through you and for you and according to God's will. You don't know what you are praying because you are not praying with your mind, but with your spirit when you pray in tongues.

> Romans 8:26-27 "And the Holy Spirit helps us in our weakness. For example, we don't know what God wants us to pray for. But the Holy Spirit prays for us with groanings that cannot be expressed in words. And the Father who knows all hearts knows what the Spirit is saying, for the

Spirit pleads for us believers in harmony with God's own will.

PRAY IMMEDIATELY

When you are sick or just feeling bad, don't wait to pray. Come to God first. Don't give him your leftovers or go to him as a last resort. I want you to get to the place where, when someone asks for prayer, you stop what you are doing and pray right away. Don't tell them, "I will pray for you," instead say, "May I pray for you right now ?" If you are just beginning, it may be all you can do to just tell someone that you will pray for them. But one day, you will be able to pray for someone face to face. It is awesome and necessary. You may be out of your comfort zone, but know that it is out of everyone's comfort zone at first. We all need practice. The more you pray out loud with someone, the more comfortable and confident you will become.

PRAY WITH FAITH

Take the leap of faith and just believe. Jesus said —

> **Mark 11:24** *"Therefore I tell you, whatever you ask for in prayer, believe that you have received it, and it will be yours."*

Prayer without faith is a useless tool/weapon. It is like having a security system installed and leaving it off because you just don't believe it actually works. My friend used to say, "Pray believing prayers or don't pray at all." When you pray, act like you just prayed. Act like you believe God heard you and is working on your behalf. So many times, we pray and then go right back to worry, fear, and doubt. Don't complain. Change your talk. Instead of complaining about how sick you are, tell yourself and others around you, "I am well; Jesus heard my prayer and has healed me. I believe I am well and this illness is running from me." Persevere, it may not seem like it, but God is working. Trust and hang in there. You are coming out victorious.

I have a book that will transform the way you pray forever. To order the book "The Acts Prayer" go to https://www.spirit filledcatholic.com/books

Also "The Miracle Hour" by Linda Schubert is a wonderful prayer formula.

21

TOOLS FOR BATTLE — PR PR PR

TURN EVERY WORRY INTO VICTORY

The following is an exercise the Holy Spirit taught me. I call it PR PR PR. It is a formula we can use to "let it go." It's easy to say, and people say it all the time. "Just let it go." But what does it mean to "let it go?" Does it mean just to drop it, or does it mean you have to deposit your fear, worry, or problem into God's hands, trusting Him to take care of it and bring it to fulfillment? This is a decision you not only have to make but then keep. This is the hard part.

The reason it is so hard is because we don't really trust God to do it. For example, our desire may be for our husband/wife to go to church and we think, "If I don't lecture him/her about it, remind them, and lay the guilt trip, who will?" Well, deep down, do we really trust God to nudge them? Do we trust the Holy Spirit to guide, draw, and convict, or do we know how to do it better than God?

Your spouse should never hear you nag or complain, and certainly never lecture. They are kings/queens, and should be treated as such. I know, I know, you may think they are losers, fat, stupid, careless, inconsiderate, disrespectful, uncaring, lazy, or worthless, but not only should those words never come out of your mouth regarding your spouse, you should never even think them. **Love conquers all, heals all, and saves all.** Love is triumphant and so are you when you choose to follow Christ and lay it down. Watch God do the job.

What are your fears, worries, concerns, and problems? Are your adult children addicted and/or away from God, are you afraid of losing your job, do you have an illness or marriage problems, or do your children have marriage problems? Are you fearful of getting cancer?

HOW do we get to the place where we can LAY IT DOWN?

1. Define your PROBLEM
2. Develop your PRAYER
3. PROCLAIM the victory

PR PR PR

- PROBLEM
- PRAYER
- PROCLAIM

This formula turns your problems into victory in three steps.

PROBLEM:

Define your problem and write it out. This helps if you are serious about letting it go. Don't just say, "I am sick," or "I need help." Be more specific: say, "My daughter is $100,000 in debt," or "My husband will not go to church, or "My son is addicted to drugs." Define your problem and write it out.

PRAYER:

General prayers generally do not get answered. "Help me" prayers are good when you are a baby Christian or desperate, but you will find God growing you up and out of that prayer really soon. Ask! God tells us over and over to ask. Ask like you believe God is listening and wants to answer your prayers. Stretch your faith and be specific when you ask.

> **Prayer example:** Father, I ask You to save my son and deliver him from these drugs that control him and have a hold on him.

> **Prayer example:** Father, I ask You to speak to my husband and draw him to you. May he join us at church and hunger and thirst for You.

THERE COMES A TIME WHEN YOU HAVE TO TAKE YOUR PRAYER TO THE NEXT LEVEL. Let's call it "Believing Prayer." Prayer that has no faith is really no prayer at all. Every prayer needs to be "Believing Prayer."

PROCLAIM:

Are you ready to bring your prayer to a whole new level of faith? This is for those of you ready to grow and mature and see breakthrough. "Proclaim" is speaking out loud the answer to your prayer as if it has already been answered. This is critical because remember in Mark 11 Jesus says, *"Have faith in God ... whatever you ask for in prayer, believe that you have received it, and it will be yours."*

Proclaim Example: My son is seeking the Lord. I have faith in God. My son is walking in wisdom and grace and is full of the Holy Spirit and free from drugs in the name of Jesus.

This is your way of showing God that you believe you have received what you asked for. Faith and trust are important to God. When we speak "I am well" we are saying it not because we feel or look well but because we believe God heard our prayer and is doing something about it. OUR FAITH is now on GOD BECAUSE WE JUST PRAYED. It is in essence faith in our prayer. It shows God you really believe He's healing you.

Here is a simple example.

- PRoblem - "I am sick."
- PRayer - "Father I come to you for healing."
- PRoclaim - "I am healed."When I say "I am well" or "I am healed,"

I believe that He is working, and I am choosing to walk by faith and not by sight (2 Cor 5:7). Proclaiming is hard at first, but so powerful. The hardest step is PROCLAIM. We do not like to proclaim something without first seeing it. Why then are we not afraid when we complain? Every time we complain, we are actually proclaiming. Unfortunately, we are proclaiming the worst-case scenario when we complain.

When we ask God to heal our son and deliver him from drugs, the last thing we want to do is complain to family and friends how bad he is. Complaining is a lack of faith. Complaining is the opposite of proclaiming, yet we are not afraid to complain at all. But we are afraid of proclaiming. Complaining is doubt, and we are not afraid to doubt; we are not afraid to express our doubt. Let's not be afraid to express our faith.

Didn't you pray? Don't you believe God is doing something? Just because you can't see Him doesn't mean He's not working, healing, delivering your son? Proclaiming changes the way we talk and, ultimately, the way we believe. How did people talk around Jesus? The woman with the issue of blood said, "If I only just touch His cloak, I will be well." The stretcher bearers probably said something like this, "If only we can get him to Jesus," and then they went through the roof. The centurion said, "Just say the word." Quit talking like God isn't working or He didn't hear you. Have faith. Show you have faith by what comes out of your mouth.

> **Example:** My son is seeking the Lord. I have faith in God. My son is walking in wisdom and grace and he is full of the Holy Spirit and free from drugs in the name of Jesus.

EVERY TIME we declare or PROCLAIM....

1. It reminds us that we have prayed.
2. It reminds us that we have laid it down.
3. It reminds us that God is working on our behalf and answering the prayer.
4. It's a reminder that we are trusting God.

It's our proclamation that proves to us and to God that we laid it down and let it go. It takes time and effort and a decision to lay it down. OUR DECLARATION keeps us on track. Our declaration or proclamation reminds us we prayed and proves our faith to God that we believe He heard us and is doing something. Our declaration/proclamation is showing God we trust in Him and have more faith in Him than in what it looks like. Our declaration shows God we have faith in Him and we believe God is working on it. Declare it every day, and you will be reminded that you have prayed, and now it's up to God. Every time you declare it you will be reminded you prayed. "Oh yeah! I prayed for this, I am confident God is working on it."

When we proclaim, we are speaking our prayer back to God as if it has already been done.

> **Mark 11:22-24** *"Jesus said to them in reply, 'Have faith in God. Amen, I say to you, whoever says to this mountain, 'Be lifted up and thrown into the sea,' and does not doubt in his heart but believes that what he says will happen, it shall be done for him. Therefore, I tell you, all that you ask for in prayer, believe that you will receive it and it shall be yours.'"*

Speak like you believe it will happen and eventually you will believe it will happen. It may seem like you are faking it or lying, but you are not lying. You just believe in something that hasn't manifested in the physical realm yet. The Bible says that faith comes by hearing. Every time you declare it you hear it.

PR PR PR - Example:

- PROBLEM - Son is addicted to drugs or alcohol.
- PRAYER - Father, I am looking to You for deliverance and freedom for my son. I am asking you to take this addiction away from him.

- PROCLAIM - My son _(add his name here)_ is hearing Your voice and turning to You. He is free from this bondage and is walking a new life following You, Lord Jesus. He has his right mind and is fully engaged in life with good friends. My son is healthy and no longer a slave to

  _____.

22

TOOLS FOR BATTLE – FAITH

J esus was amazed at the faith of the sick woman, the faith of the Canaanite woman, and the faith of the Centurion. Jesus will be surprised at your faith in Him as well.

The SICK WOMAN -

Mark 5:34 *He said to her, "Daughter, your faith has saved you. Go in peace and be cured of your affliction."*

The CANAANITE WOMAN -

Matthew 15:28 *Then Jesus said to her in reply, "O woman, great is your faith! Let it be done for you as you wish." And her daughter was healed at that hour.*

The CENTURION -

Matthew 8:10 *When Jesus heard this, he was amazed and said to those following him, "Amen, I say to you, in no one in Israel have I found such faith.*

Be bold as you come to God for prayer. Be like a little child asking his or her mommy or daddy to kiss it and make it better. That little child does not doubt his/her parents' desire to fix it. Why do we doubt God's desire to make it all better for us, His children? He wants us to approach Him like you want your little children to approach you, with confidence that you not only can, but will. Imagine waking your son up in the morning and finding him in bed with a festering wound, and he says, "Oh, Mom/Dad, I didn't want to bother you." How would you feel?

God cares about everything, even about the little things.

I Peter 5:7 *"Cast all your cares on me because I care for you."*

Learn to do it. Practice it today. Cast your cares on Jesus. He can handle it. You cannot handle it, but He can. Practice with the little things, and when the big one comes, you will be ready because you will know who to go to, and you will go with confidence like David did. David wasn't afraid of Goliath as he had killed the bear and the lion while he tended the sheep. God wants ALL your cares, not just some of them.

John 14:12-14"*I tell you the truth, anyone who has faith in Me will do what I have been doing. He will do even greater things than these, because I am going to the Father. And I will do whatever you ask in My name, so that the Son may bring glory to the Father. You may ask Me for anything in my name, and I will do it.*"

God has a message for you. He loves you and cares about you. Sometimes it is so hard to believe God cares and is working on our behalf, especially when the prayer isn't answered right away. You may have to wait a short while or a long while, but He is working. Trust that the wait will be worth it.

23

TOOLS FOR BATTLE – LOVE AND FORGIVENESS

Love covers a multitude of sins, the Bible says. God's love is beyond our human understanding. He gave us His love so we can love and forgive others. We have no excuse if the love of God lives in us. We are capable of loving ONLY because of His love for us. God loved us first, and because of that, we have everything it takes to love. Have you ever noticed how much easier it is to love someone who first loves you? It's so much more difficult to love those who come against you. God made it easy for us. We first have to receive and believe in His love for us.

God's love is empowering. God is the source of love. Without God as the center of our lives we can only love ourselves. We may act like we love others or it may look like we are loving and kind, but without God we cannot love others. He is love.

1 John 4:19 *"We love because he first loved us."*

Love and forgiveness go hand in hand. When you forgive, you are expressing love in its highest form. When you forgive you act just like Jesus. When we forgive we show off Jesus; we represent Him and He is glorified through us. Don't be offended or allow yourself to become bitter and resentful. Just because we hurt doesn't mean we have the right to withhold love and forgiveness. God gives us love unconditionally and expects us to love back in the same way. The devil has no hold on us when we love and forgive. We rule through love. We are powerful in love and forgiveness.

I know you are thinking, "How dare she expect me to forgive that one person? She doesn't know what happened or how horrific it was." I don't know, but God knows and He cares and He weeps with you. And He still expects forgiveness from you. Let God have that person. Let God determine their future. God wants you free from all the side-effects of unforgiveness.

Corrie Ten Boom, a Dutch woman who survived the Nazi concentration camp where she was sent for hiding Jews in her home during World War II, was speaking at a little church in Munich, Germany. She spoke about God's forgiveness and mercy and all she experienced in the concentration camp. After the service a man in a grey overcoat walked up to her. She recognized him immediately as he approached. He was her enemy. He was one of the cruel guards at that very same camp.

> *She said, "I was face-to-face with one of my captors and my blood seemed to freeze." He said to her,*
>
> *"You mentioned Ravensbruck in your talk, I was a guard there. But since that time, I have become a Christian. I know that God has forgiven me for the cruel things I did there, but I*

would like to hear it from your lips as well. Fräulein, will you forgive me?"

"And I stood there... with the coldness clutching my heart. But forgiveness is not an emotion — I knew that too. Forgiveness is an act of the will, and the will can function regardless of the temperature of the heart.".

"'Help!' I prayed silently. 'I can lift my hand. I can do that much. You supply the feeling.' And so woodenly, mechanically, I thrust my hand into the one stretched out to me. And as I did, an incredible thing took place. The current started in my shoulder, raced down my arm, sprang into our joined hands. And then this healing warmth seemed to flood my whole being, bringing tears to my eyes. 'I forgive you, brother!' I cried. 'With all my heart!' For a long moment we grasped each other's hands, the former guard and the former prisoner. I had never known God's love so intensely, as I did then" (an excerpt from www. familylifeeducation.org)

You are of the same noble birth. The same current runs through you. You are a man or woman of integrity. You are strong in the Lord and a child of God. Just obey and watch God take care of the feelings and everything else. God does not leave us alone to fend for ourselves. He is with us on the front lines.

Forgiveness is an act of the will, and the will can function regardless of the temperature of the heart.
Corrie Ten Boom

Forgiveness doesn't mean you have to be reconciled with the person who hurt you. You don't have to have a relationship with them. You don't have to visit them or meet with them, or ever even see them again. It doesn't even mean you have to say, "I forgive you." Forgiveness is internal. Something between you and God alone. If the Holy Spirit wants you to tell the person you forgive them, one day, He will let you know. If you are in the middle of something volatile or dangerous - get out. Forgiveness does not mean staying there.

Forgiveness simply means making the decision to stop holding their sin against them. It means you decide to quit blaming them. You are releasing them from having to pay you back in some way or make things right. Forgiveness is releasing the person into God's hands.

The feeling of anger or outrage may not leave immediately, but it will. God will do that work in you. God expects us to love our enemies. So make that decision. Just say, today I chose to love and forgive.

> **Matthew 5:43-44** *"You have heard the commandment, 'You shall love your countryman but hate your enemy.' My command to you is: love your enemies."*

God will take care of that person who hurt you or offends you. Trust Him. Don't take matters into your own hands and don't even think negatively about that person anymore. God promises justice for everyone who wrongs you. TRUST HIM.

> **Romans 12:17-21** *" Do not repay anyone evil for evil; be concerned for what is noble in the sight of all. [18] If possible, on your part, live at peace with all. [19] Beloved, do not look for revenge but leave room for the wrath; for it is written, 'Vengeance is mine, I will repay, says the Lord.' [20] Rather, 'if*

your enemy is hungry, feed him; if he is thirsty, give him some-
thing to drink; for by so doing you will heap burning coals upon
his head.' 21 Do not be conquered by evil but conquer evil with
good."

The devil loves when you get offended and withhold forgiveness because you act and sound just like he does. Unforgiveness opens the door to demonic activity in your life. It is an invitation to bitterness and resentment and full-blown sin and sickness and death. In the same way, forgiveness opens the door to healing and life.

We revel in unforgiveness as if it is our right. We believe we are justified. Some of us love our "VICTIM" Status. We have been the victim for so long, complaining and talking about it, that we don't know any other way. We become comfortable being the one who was hurt. Poor pitiful me. Our unforgiveness becomes a monument to our pain. Well, today is the day you decide to forgive and tear down this idol.

Love and forgiveness never fail (1 Corinthians 13:8).

I challenge you to forgive the everyday things your family and friends do that hurt. Forgive and forgive quickly. Don't dwell on it. Nip it in the bud. Be purposeful. Be brave and make the decision to love even when it seems impossible. You can do the impossible through Christ Jesus. You can do it! Without Him it's impossible to forgive someone who hurt you but you are more than a mere human. You are filled with Holy Spirit and Jesus lives in you. You are made in His image and through Him you can do anything and everything. Nothing is too difficult for you, including and especially forgiveness.

Forgive and forgive quickly those nasty comments that make you want to bite back. Forgive bad service, friends or family members forgetting your birthday, or that someone who ignored you or neglected to mention you. Forgive those who overlook your hard work or neglect your feelings. Forgive the person walking by who did not smile. Be like God.

- DO IT - as often as you are hurt by comments -
- DO IT QUICKLY - don't let something start to brew
- DO IT DAILY - make it your new way of life

His power is in you so you can do it. You have no excuse. It's time to rise up and be the man or woman of God you were called and anointed to be.

When you forgive you will receive:

- Sense of peace
- Sense of accomplishment
- Restored relationship
- Freedom from guilt
- FREEDOM
- Sense of integrity
- Sense of Power
- Sense of satisfaction
- Victory

Forgiveness is simply a decision. Think of unforgiveness as a series of negative thoughts. JUST thoughts. You can change your thoughts. You can change your mind. Make a decision for the Lord's sake. Don't do it for the person you need to forgive; do it for your sake. Do if for the Lord. You may not feel like or want to, but make the decision to forgive them whether you feel like it or not. Do it for God's sake and He will reward you. Think of your forgiveness as a gift to God. It will not go unnoticed. God wants for you freedom from your hurt and pain and it comes through you forgiving.

ARE YOU READY?

Repeat after me.

> "God, I am willing. I don't feel like it but I want to do this for You; to honor You. I want to forgive and keep on forgiving. I want to be a forgiver, a lover, a believer. I don't want to grow bitter and hateful. I choose Your way, not mine. I choose to obey You because I love You Father. I want to do this as a way of saying thank You for loving me and forgiving me."

Don't wait until you feel like it. The feelings will come. Trust God with the feelings. Begin wherever you are today. You may not want to forgive, but do something. Make this your prayer to God. Say something like, "Lord, I want to forgive, help me to want to forgive _____(name). I can't do it now but I want to do your will."

Maybe all you can say right now is, "I want to want to forgive." Or, "I want to want to want to forgive."

24

TOOLS FOR BATTLE – YOUR MOUTH

Psalm 18:2-4 "I love you, Lord, my strength,
Lord, my rock, my fortress, my deliverer,
My God, my rock of refuge, my shield, my
saving horn, my stronghold! Praised be
the Lord, I exclaim! I have been delivered
from my enemies."

YOUR WORDS ARE POWERFUL

Every time thoughts come, we have an opportunity to speak. Our words are powerful: words can build up or destroy. We spend a lot of time saying, "I'm tired, I'm sick." We want people (especially our family members) to feel sorry for us; we say, "I am going to die." We tell our friends how bad things are. We want them to know what we are going through; we want them to do something for us, to make it better and save us. Why is it so easy to say, "I am sick," or, I am sick of this or that," instead of, "I am so blessed?"

Let's spend some time saying the opposite. What do we have to lose?

Instead say, "I am well."

You may not feel well, but you are speaking faith in your God who heard your prayers. Breaking bad habits is hard. We have made a habit of the way we talk. It takes practice to break these habits. At first, it will sound weird saying the opposite of what you feel.

You have to say something.

There is power in your words to convince yourself and your enemy of who you are trusting. Say, "I am trusting my Father to pull me through." Your mood won't change unless you do something to change it. Your anger won't subside if you keep feeding it by thinking about it or talking and complaining.

SPEAKING TO YOURSELF IS AN ACTION!!

IT IS YOU TAKING ACTION.

God can't resist your faith in Him. SAY, "I trust You, Jesus." Say it, and eventually, you will start believing it. Tell God the same thing David said above in Psalm 18:

"You are my Rock, Lord, my fortress, my deliverer, my God, my rock of refuge, my shield, my saving horn, my stronghold! Praised be the Lord, I exclaim! I have been delivered from my enemies."

Your words are key. Say it until you believe what you are saying is true. It's a choice. You can stay quiet and stay depressed, angry, worried, fearful, and offended, or speak and change your heart. God can't help you get out unless you want Him to.

Prove to God you are serious by learning His word and by letting it come out of your mouth.

Our minds need to be renewed. We can't keep thinking as we have always thought and believe something different. We can't keep speaking as we've always spoken and expect things to change. We need to shake off the old and put on Christ. We need to talk to ourselves and convince ourselves that we are brand new creatures in Christ and then something brand new is going to happen to us and in us. We are not just physical beings, we are spiritual as well. That is how we are "IN CHRIST." It's spiritual.

Speak to the Mountains/Strongholds

> **Mark11:22–25** *"Have faith in God," Jesus answered. "Truly I tell you, if anyone says to this mountain, 'Go, throw yourself into the sea,' and does not doubt in their heart but believes that what they say will happen, it will be done for them. Therefore I tell you, whatever you ask for in prayer, believe that you have received it, and it will be yours.And when you stand praying, if you hold anything against anyone, forgive them, so that your Father in heaven may forgive you your sins."*

What mountain is in your way? What stronghold is looming in your thought life, in your dreams? What mountain or mountains do you need to throw into the sea, never to be remembered or revisited? I don't mean the beautiful, majestic mountains we all wish we lived next to. I mean those huge, crushing, overpowering, overwhelming mountains or circumstances. They may be memories, disease, sin, fear, worry, debt, finances, cancer, alcohol, addiction, anger, or unforgiveness.

What mountain needs to be uprooted and thrown into the sea? Is it the memory of an event, a sin, depression, or marriage problems? What seems insurmountable or impossible? What is troubling you beyond your ability to conquer or overcome? Maybe your mountain is a bunch of things, and you can't quite name what is bothering you. You just feel oppressed. You feel dread and doom as if something is looming over you.

A mountain is something we can't see over or around or get across to the other side. A mountain is something standing in your way to freedom and the good life Jesus promised. The mountain is always there. If it isn't in front of you, it is following behind you. You see it wherever you go; it's something you can't get away from. A mountain is a stronghold that needs to be demolished.

It's time to talk to our mountains and take them down. Jesus advised, "SAY to this mountain." Jesus expects us to speak to our mountain and He expects something to be done about it. I once heard someone say this, "**We talk to God about how big our mountains are, but we should be talking to our mountains about how big our God is.**"

This is so true. We talk to God and each other about how horrible our problems are when we should be talking to our problems about how great our God is! Let's refocus. Once we begin telling our problems what a great big God we have, our problems will seem small and manageable in comparison.

Jesus spoke about a mountain because He wants us to know that He is the God of the impossible. It is impossible to move a mountain in the natural world we live in. IMPOSSIBLE. But Jesus says that if we believe, nothing is impossible, not even moving a mountain with a word. Our faith is remarkable, powerful and can move even a mountain. Jesus used the extreme because he wanted to make a point. NOTHING IS IMPOSSIBLE IF YOU BELIEVE (Mark 9:23).

If you are dealing with cancer, here is a way to address this mountain:

> *Cancer, my God is greater, my God is stronger, my God is higher than you or anything you can throw at me; my God is healer, awesome in power, and nothing is too difficult for Him.*

YOU CAN talk to your mountains. Jesus said so. Our words are powerful and can build up or destroy, no matter how big, how oppressive, how imposing, how ugly. You CAN talk and defeat that mountain of fear and move that mountain of insecurity. You may think you deserve that mountain of trouble, but it is time for it to go. You may have sinned and earned the pain you are going through, but you don't have to remain this way. Jesus came to take your sins and set you free from all its consequences and guilt and shame.

> **Mark 11:23** *"'Have Faith in God ,' Jesus answered, 'Truly I tell you, if anyone says to this mountain, 'Go, throw yourself into the sea,' and does not doubt in their heart but believes that what they say will happen, it will be done for them.'"*

Now let's practice. Tell your problems to throw themselves into the sea.

> **Insecurity, go throw yourself into the sea.Fear, go throw yourself into the sea.Depression, go throw yourself into the sea. Sickness or disease, go throw yourself into the**

sea. Resentment, bitterness, anxiety/worry, addictions, jealousy — go throw yourself into the sea!

Now believe it! Jesus goes on to say, *"Therefore I tell you, whatever you ask for in prayer, believe that you have received it, and it will be yours"* (**Mark 11:24**).

Believe that God has heard your prayers. Believe that He is on your side, that He is fighting your battles for you. Believe that whatever you ask for in prayer you have received (see section on Faith).

Start speaking to God the moment you wake up. What comes out of your mouth influences what you think and how you feel. The devil wants you to feel bad and to expect the worst, and he is ready to go the minute you wake up. You may feel scared, nervous, or sick when you wake up, but do not receive those thoughts and accept them. Begin by speaking the opposite. Start with a memorized scripture. *"The Lord is my shepherd. There is nothing I lack."* (**Psalm 23:1.**)

Psalm 16:8 "I have set the LORD always before me. Because He is at my right hand, I will not be shaken."

What you say when you open your eyes is very important. It will make or break your day. Every morning when you wake up you have to speak to yourself and minister to yourself. This is a must. Don't let the devil tell you how you feel and what you think and believe today.

You tell you. Let the Holy Spirit tell you. Don't let the circumstances or events of yesterday or the coming days determine your mood or attitude. You decide the moment you wake up what you believe. Don't listen to your feelings or the thoughts the devil is sending your way. Let your words determine your feelings. Watch your feelings and your attitude change within minutes as you speak.

LET THE DEVIL RUN IN FEAR OF YOU every morning. When your feet hit the floor imagine snuffing him out. Imagine him a pesky insect, or even better, dried leaves under your feet.

SAY

"I am Your child, Lord, and today is a good day. I am blessed, healthy, and filled with the Holy Spirit. I am not only blessed but will be a blessing. I am Your precious child. I am in charge of my thoughts and my mood, and therefore I command every thought into obedience to You, Lord Jesus. My mind is in perfect peace because I rest in You, Lord. I am happy and content today because You, Lord Jesus, are my Lord and Savior and You are with me and watching over me and have already delivered me from every evil. I will not fear. Instead I will trust in You. I am Yours, and I declare Your love for me. I believe in Your love for me and receive it. I will not listen to doubt or fear for I know You are with me, and You command your angels to surround, comfort, and protect me. I am healthy and well, and sickness is far from me because by Your stripes, Lord Jesus, I am healed. The spirit of infirmity is under my feet. I am healthy and well because You took all my sins and sickness. I can do all things today through Christ who strengthens me."

> Ephesians 1:3 *"All praise to God, the Father of our Lord Jesus Christ, who has blessed us with every spiritual blessing in the heavenly realms because we are united with Christ." – NLT*

Give glory to the Lord. The devil hates it. He hates to hear you talk about God's goodness and make any declarations of faith. Remember we walk and talk and live by faith, not by feelings. We walk by faith, not by sight, the Bible says in 2 Corinthians 5:7. When you speak, you are speaking the truth. You may not feel well, but say it anyway. It may not feel like the truth, but you are speaking the truth. We are speaking forth truths based on God's Word, His promises to us, not on our feelings. We are declaring what God says about us, His plan for us, His will for us. We aren't waiting until we can see it in the physical. We are choosing to believe it before we see it. We want Him to know we believe He is in control of the situation and fighting on our behalf.

The truth is Jesus conquered sin and sickness and took it with Him to the cross (Matthew 8:17), so you are speaking the truth when you say, "I am well."

The truth is God has plans for us, plans to prosper us, plans for a future full of hope (Jeremiah 29:11). Now believe it and believe it's for you also.

25

TOOLS FOR BATTLE - THE WORD OF GOD

The Word of God is powerful. God made heaven and earth with just a word. Jesus Himself is the Word of God made flesh. The Word of God is living and active, true, established and fixed. The Word of God is forever trustworthy, life-giving, and health to one's whole being. The Word is GOD HIMSELF.

> **John 1:14** *"And the Word became flesh and made his dwelling among us"*
>
> **Proverbs 4:20-22** *"My son, pay attention to my words, listen carefully to the words I say; don't let them out of your sight, keep them deep in your heart. They are life to those who grasp them, health for the entire body."*

Read God's word. It was meant to be read. Read with the Holy Spirit and bring a notebook because if you are listening, God is speaking. If you don't read God's word how will know what He has for you, what He wants for you, what He says to you and about you, and all His promises for you?

In Ephesians, Chapter 6, God says to put on the armor of God and take the sword of the Spirit which is the Word of God. The Word of God is powerful because it has the force of heaven behind it.

> **2 Corinthians 10:3–4** *"For though we live in the world, we do not wage war as the world does. The weapons we fight with are not the weapons of the world. On the contrary, they have divine power to demolish strongholds.*

The Word of God is sharper than any double-edged sword. So, imagine what damage it is doing to the kingdom of darkness (Hebrews 4:12). No wonder the devil hates to hear it. Let's bother the devil today.

> **2 Corinthians 10:5** *"We demolish arguments and every pretension that sets itself up against the knowledge of God, and we take captive every thought to make it obedient to Christ."*

COMMAND the Devil's whisperings to leave in the name of Jesus. Make your thoughts obey God. Just do it. Put your hands on your head and say, "I COMMAND my thoughts into obedience." When you start obsessing or thinking that your husband is unfaithful, or your children are going to get sick and die — put your hands on your head and command your mind. Say, "Mind, I command you to obey Jesus." We have weapons at our disposal that are powerful and can pull down strongholds. Our weapons are supernatural, and they are mighty and real and victorious.

Our weapon is the Word of God and it is ours to use against the enemy. Depression is the enemy. It is defeatable because it's already been defeated. Cancer is the enemy and it's defeated. Addiction is the enemy and it's defeated and conquered. You cannot fight it alone and you cannot fight it lying down hoping it will just retreat and leave you alone.

Pray Scripture.

Much of Scripture is prayer. Did you know that we can use Scripture and make it our own personal prayer? God's Word is true and perfect and a great way to pray. When we pray God's word it shows God we believe in Him and His word, and we believe His Word is true and powerful. You can never pray wrong when you pray God's Word back to Him. How can He refuse? When we pray God's Word, we know we are praying according to His will for us.

Personalize the scriptures below by filling in your name or the name of the person you are praying for.

Psalm 91 is a great Scripture passage to pray. The whole Psalm is a prayer. I am including the first few verses and how to pray them.

> *(Verse 1) Whoever dwells in the shelter of the Most High will rest in the shadow of the Almighty.* Father I am Yours and You are my shelter in the storm, I choose to rest in You.

> *(Verse 2) I will say of the LORD, "He is my refuge and my fortress, my God, in whom I trust."* You Lord are my refuge, my fortress, nothing can hurt me. I trust You, God.

> (Verse 3) *Surely He will save you from the fowler's snare and from the deadly pestilence.* Surely, You will save me from every trap the enemy sets for me. You will surely save me from sickness and disease and EVERY LITTLE THOUGHT that comes into my head. Thank you for

keeping me from harm. I am not afraid of anything. Nothing can harm me because I am in Your care.

Colossians 1:9–10 Pray this for a loved one.

> *(Verse 9) We continually ask God to fill you with the knowledge of His will through all the wisdom and understanding that the Spirit gives ...* God, I ask you to fill ___(the name of a person in need)___with the knowledge of Your will. Give him/her wisdom and understanding so that ____may live a life worthy of You Lord.

> *(Verse 10) so that you may live a life worthy of the Lord and please him in every way: bearing fruit in every good work, growing in the knowledge of God.* I pray that _____ will please You in every way and that he/she will bear fruit as he/she works and grows in the knowledge of You, Lord.

All of Colossians is a prayer. How serious are you about growing in God's grace? How much time do you have? Make it your prayer and pray a couple verses a day.

When you wake up in the morning, proclaim God's word out loud no matter how you feel. The moment you wake up say,

> **"By his stripes, I am healed. I trust You, Lord Jesus. I am well. Thank you, Lord, for taking my sicknesses and diseases."**

You may not be feeling well, but your feelings are not the truth, the word of God is the truth. Say this and think on these things.

Don't let your thoughts go wild. They will try to run down a certain path, but you are in charge. Remind yourself who God is and that you belong to Him, and He loves you. Remind yourself that He sent His son to die for you. Remember that He took with him to the cross all your sins and all your diseases.

> **Psalm 103:3** *"Who pardons all your sins and heals all your diseases..."*

> **Psalm 91:9-11** *"Because you have made the highest your stronghold, no evil shall befall you, no affliction come near your tent. For he commands his angels concerning you, to guard you wherever you go."*

Believe God's Word more than what you feel. More than what it looks like or seems like or what the world thinks. God rescued you from all evil and all darkness and all sin and all the consequences of sin through His Son Jesus. God sent Jesus to rescue you. When you have cancer – God wants you well. When you have pneumonia – God wants you well. When you have depression – God wants you well. When you have anxiety – God wants you well.

Repeat aloud after me, "God wants me well, He loves me and cares about me."

26

TOOLS FOR BATTLE – JESUS

J ESUS IS OUR STRONGHOLD

Without Jesus, we are at the mercy of principalities, and spiritual forces of evil. With Jesus we are more than conquerors.

Our stronghold as Christians should be Jesus Christ. The Word of God says, "He is our stronghold" (Psalm 18:2). He makes us strong and immovable, unshakable, trustworthy noble men and women of integrity, true men and women of God. How is Jesus our Stronghold? Listen to what the Word of God says about Jesus.

1. – Jesus said, "I am the Way, the Truth and the Life, no one comes to the Father except through me" (John 14:6).

2. – God says that "everyone who calls on the name of the Lord will be saved" (Romans 10:13).

3. – God tells us, "For the wages of sin is death, but the gift of God is eternal life in Christ Jesus our Lord" (Romans 6:24).

4. – God says, "And who can win this battle against the world? Only those who believe that Jesus is the Son of God." 1 John 5:5

5. – Jesus saves us perfectly, since He lives forever interceding for us. God says, "Therefore He is also able to save to the uttermost those who come to God through Him, since He always lives to make intercession for them" (Hebrews 7:25).

There may be an ongoing battle for us and for our minds, but with Jesus as Lord, we win. Jesus is alive! Jesus is our Lord and Savior. Without Jesus as our Lord and Savior, we are at the mercy of principalities and spiritual forces of evil in the heavenly realms. With Jesus we are more than conquerors and we can overcome anything. We are no longer trapped, no longer stuck, and no longer enslaved, but free.

Commitment to Jesus as Lord and Savior

Are you ready to trust Jesus with your life? Are you ready to choose Jesus as your Lord and Savior?

You have to choose Jesus for yourself at some point.

The following quote comes from the Christ Renews His Parish (CHRP) Manual, ("Christ Renews His Parish" is a spiritual renewal program the Catholic Church offered for many years.) "Christianity did not begin with a theological formulation, a set of laws, or even a prayer form; it certainly did not begin with a document. It began with a person. Christianity is all about commitment to a person, the person of Jesus Christ. Jesus says, "Here I am, I stand at the door and knock. If anyone hears my voice and opens the door, I will come in."

The manual also says, "The act of commitment is a prayer of self-offering, which in simple terms expresses belief in Christ as Savior and Lord, acknowledges our sinfulness and need, and clearly places our entire life in the hands of Jesus." It goes on to say, "Being a follower of Jesus is not a matter of birth, but of decision... The tradition of infant baptism claims the faith of the community for the infant but expects each to choose Jesus for himself when he can do so."

My conversion experience came when I was twenty-nine. At the time, I wanted to change the world; I thought I could make a difference in the world and be a champion for the poor. I expected so much more from my life than merely existing and accumulating wealth, and I was filled with guilt and shame. I thought I should be in the Peace Corps or on the mission field instead of making money and spending it on myself. I was racked with guilt. One night, God met me and spoke to me. I heard his voice like peaceful thunder. I heard it everywhere, yet probably not audibly, and He said, "Come to Me first, and then you will have the power."

He said, "Come to Me first, and then you will have the power."

It was as if all of a sudden, the lights went on. I remember screaming YES, YES, over and over again. Those amazing words from God opened my eyes to His awesome love for me for the first time. I heard and immediately gave my life to Him. I said YES, and have never been the same since, nor have I turned back. I became a new person deep down inside me. I had grown up Catholic, went to Catholic schools, and received all the sacraments with knowledge and enthusiasm, and I genuinely loved God. But that day I surrendered my life to him. All my life I was trying to do good and earn his love, but all He wanted was me.

The reality of that is still being revealed to me to this day. He wanted ME, and He wanted me just the way I was: a sinner, used, defiled, and ugly. I didn't deserve him; I didn't deserve His mercy, I had an affair with a married man, an abortion, and much more. I didn't deserve his mercy, yet he extended to me not only mercy and forgiveness but a job in His KING-DOM, a seat with him, partnership, and a place at his table. He was giving me His name, choosing me as His child! He was willing to invest in me because I was worth it to Him.

He didn't expect me to come to him all clean and pretty; He wanted me just the way I was (THIS IS MIND BLOWING). He didn't say, "First go to confession, and then I'll take you." No! He wanted me right then and there just as I was, dirt and all; sin and all.

I matter to Him. It will take a lifetime to clean me up and mold me into His image. That night He stood at the door of my heart and knocked, and I opened it.

He made it so clear to me as if He was saying, "Your itty, bitty way or MINE!" I realized in that instant that what I was trying to accomplish on my own was possible only with Him. What a partnership He was offering me. That night the God of the universe, the omnipotent all-powerful God, was standing at the door of my heart waiting for my response (little 'ole me). God considered me worthy of His time and attention. My response was a resounding YES. That night I was forever changed because I made a commit-ment to Him. I said "Yes." God stopped everything for me.

That is what it felt like. He was standing there waiting for my answer. I felt so special that night.

Jesus is here right now and is calling you. You are not reading this by accident. Jesus is saying,

> *"Here I am, I stand at the door and knock. If anyone hears my voice and opens the door I will come in"* (**Rev. 3:20**).

We can make a commitment to our church, to our community, to the poor, and even to those in prison, but it will not gain us anything in the sight of God without a personal commitment to Jesus Christ, His Son, our Lord, and Savior. So what does it mean to accept Jesus as Lord and Savior? First, what does it mean to make Jesus Lord?

Jesus as Lord

God made Jesus Lord of heaven and earth because Jesus lowered Himself to accept death, death on a cross. Jesus gave God His innocent blood in exchange for our guilty blood. He took our guilt so we could be cleansed and made pure and holy in God's sight. For this reason, God exalted Him as Lord.

> **Philippians 2:10** *"At the name of Jesus every knee shall bow and every tongue proclaim Jesus Christ is Lord.*

It will happen one day. One day everyone will bow. Better now than later when it's too late.

With Jesus as Lord, all things are ours. If your past haunts you, you have the opportunity in Christ to begin again. No matter how old you are, no matter how long you have done things your way, you have the opportunity to begin again and turn your life over to Jesus. Let Him manage your life. Let Him be in charge of you. Let Him be Lord.

Often, we hear, "I came home to the church," or "I finally came back to the church," or "I found church for the first time." But salvation is found in Jesus Christ, not in a church building and not in a denomination, but in the person of Jesus Christ. We worship Jesus, not a church.

When we come to Jesus as our Lord, our whole life will be turned around, true healing, forgiveness, freedom, and life is ours. Jesus says, "*I came that they may have life and have it abundantly*" (**John 10:10**). He wasn't lying. His way leads us to the good life. He is not keeping it from us but offering it to us here on earth. We can trust Him as Lord because He is faithful and true, perfect and trustworthy. He knows more than you do. He cares about you more than you do.

When we commit to Jesus as Lord, we surrender our right to do things our way. He becomes Lord; He is in control. His way for our way. What an exchange! The perfect for the imperfect. We are billions of beings walking around on earth in charge of our own lives, thinking we know what is best for us.

The problem is that everybody has a different idea and formula for life. God is saying to each of us on earth, "Here I am, ask Me, I know." God is perfect, and His will for our lives is perfect. He wants only the best for us. When we give our lives to Christ, what do we get in return? Everything! All God's promises are ours. Jesus said, "*Seek first the Kingdom of heaven and His righteousness and all these things will be added to you as well*" (**Matthew 6:33**). Everything you need and desire, God will provide for you.

2 Corinthians 1:20 *"For all of God's promises have been fulfilled in Christ with a resounding 'Yes!'"*

WHAT? What does that mean; all of God's promises are ours? What promises? Every promise God ever made to Israel in the Old Testament is ours!

Promises such as...

- "Your towns and your fields will be blessed.
- Your children and your crops will be blessed.
- The offspring of your herds and flocks will be blessed.
- Your fruit baskets and breadboards will be blessed.
- Wherever you go and whatever you do, you will be blessed.
- The Lord will conquer your enemies when they attack you. They will attack you from one direction, but they will scatter from you in seven!"
  Deuteronomy 28:3-7

Jesus fulfilled the entire Old Testament for us. He worked out our salvation for us. This is why it's called Good news. Jesus became the spotless pure lamb of God for us. (See Chapter "Someone Had to Die" for more)

> **Ephesians 1:3** *"All praise to God, the Father of our Lord Jesus Christ, who has blessed us with every spiritual blessing in the heavenly realms because we are united with Christ."*

How do we make Jesus our Lord? What do I do? First of all, Jesus is Lord of everything!!! God made it so. He already is Lord; you just have to come to Him and submit to His Lordship. He is Lord whether you submit to him as Lord or not. Choose Jesus now.

HOW? The Bible tells us how in the Scripture below. Confess with your mouth that Jesus is Lord. Tell someone. Speak. Join a church and hang out with other believers. Get Baptized. Do something. Make it real. Confessing with your mouth makes it real.

> **Romans 10:9–13** *"For, if you confess with your mouth that Jesus is Lord and believe in your heart that God raised him from the dead, you will be saved. For one believes with the heart and so is justified, and one confesses with the mouth and so is saved. For the scripture says, 'No one who believes in him will be put to shame.' For there is no distinction between Jew and Greek; the same Lord is Lord of all, enriching all who call upon him. For "everyone who calls on the name of the Lord will be saved."*

Ask the Holy Spirit for help

The Holy Spirit gives you the power to make Jesus Lord. The Holy Spirit gives you the power to commit your life to Jesus. The Holy Spirit gives us the power to live for Him also. He doesn't leave us on our own. We can't begin to live for Jesus without the Holy Spirit and we can't continue to live for Jesus without the Holy Spirit. He keeps us "In Christ."

Now let's talk about Jesus as Savior.

Jesus as Savior

The Bible says, *"If righteousness could be gained through the law then Christ died for nothing"* (**Galatians 2:21**). If we can be made right with God by obeying all the commandments, then Christ died for nothing. If we could save ourselves, then we don't need a savior.

We want to be righteous; we want to be made right with God. We want to be free from sins and sinfulness, but we can't do it on our own. That is why we need a savior, and that is why God sent His Son. God knew we needed a Savior. When we accept Jesus as our Savior, we accept that what He did on the cross was for us personally. We believe that our sins are on Him. We believe His death meant something. We believe He died for us and that the punishment we deserved for our sins, he took for us. His death was payment in full for every sin ever committed in the whole world.

You have an opportunity to make a radical decision for Christ that will forever change your life. For some of us that may have already happened. God made a covenant with us and signed it with the blood of Jesus. *"This cup is the new covenant in my blood which is poured out for you"* (**Luke 22:20**). Jesus gave it all for us, and now He stands at the door and knocks. Jesus gave His blood for us on a cross so that God would keep the Covenant. God made a New Covenant with Jesus, His life in exchange for our forgiveness and eternal life. It is ours through this Covenant God made with us through Jesus Christ. Jesus became a man to represent us and die for us.

> **Ephesians 3:12** *"In him and through faith in him we may approach God with freedom and confidence."*

There are other ways to God but only one sure way. Any other way and we are trusting in ourselves to get to heaven. We are counting on our own goodness or our ability to obey the laws to bring us to heaven. We will always fail. It's impossible on our own. It is impossible to get to heaven on our own. God knew this from the beginning.

When our confidence is in our own strength, it is weak at best. We will always wonder, never sure if God hears us. Because of Jesus, I can enter God's personal quarters in heaven boldly and with confidence, and so can you because He took our sins away completely and forever. Jesus made us pure. Jesus made us brand new, white as snow, cleansed.

We not only can enter God's throne room, but we do so with assurance that we belong. We can approach God boldly because we trust in Jesus' offering completely. We believe He died for us and was buried and took our sins with Him. We go confidently because we believe our sins have been forgiven and washed away, so there is nothing keeping us from GOD! Jesus made us His brothers and sisters, and we can run to our Daddy knowing He accepts us. We do so with joy and peace, all because of Jesus.

27

TOOLS FOR BATTLE – PRAISE

W hen we praise God, something supernatural happens. Ask the people of Jericho, who watched as the entire wall surrounding the city fell when the people began to shout (See Joshua Chapter 6). Ask the people of Israel what happened to the enemy troops advancing against them when they began to sing.

> **2 Chronicles 20:22** *"When they began to sing, the Lord threw the invading armies into a panic."*

Do you want victory over strongholds in your life? Begin praising God.

What does it mean to PRAISE GOD?

- **Praise is** being preoccupied with GOD, with who He is and what He has done.
- **Praise is** raising much ado about God.
- **Praise is** giving God the GLORY.

The freedictionary.com defines praise as "to commend, to applaud, to express approval of, or admiration of, to extol in words or song, to magnify, to glorify, to exalt." Praise is extolling, magnifying, glorifying and exalting God. Praise is telling others about God, who He is or what He has done for you.

Why Do We NEED To Praise God?

The Bible commands us to praise the Lord over and over again. Why? Why does God want us to praise Him? Does He need it? Does it give Him a thrill or make Him feel good about Himself? Does God have an ego? Why do we praise God and why does God tell us to praise Him in the Bible?

We praise God because WE need it. PRAISE brings us into a new world, a new realm; the spiritual realm.

When we magnify God, our troubles begin to pale in comparison. When we talk about how great God is, we start to believe it. God wants us to hear ourselves praising Him because our words are powerful. Our words change our minds, our moods, and our attitudes. He wants others to hear us praising Him as well because He wants us and others to remember just how awesome He is. He wants us to remember this in times of trouble so we will know where to go and to whom.

> **Psalm 145:11-12** "*They speak of the glory of your reign and tell of your mighty works, making known to the sons of men your mighty acts, the majestic glory of your rule.*"

Praise is telling God how great He is. For instance, the Bible says that God is our "Ever present help in time of need" (Psalm 46). The Bible describes God as all-knowing, all-powerful, our healer and defender. God doesn't tell us He is all powerful just to brag; He tells us He is all-powerful so we will trust Him to fight for us. He tells us He is our defender, so we can count on him defending us. He tells us He heals not to impress us, but so we will trust Him to heal us. God tells us how great and mighty He is for our sake.

God wants to hear those words of praise coming out of our mouths because He knows that faith comes from hearing. When we speak it, we hear it. Eventually, we will start believing the words we are speaking. The Bible describes God as our ever-present help in our time of need because He is. He means it. He doesn't want us to doubt His love and ability and willingness to help us. He wants us to count on it. He wants us to tell others how great He is so others will know where to go for help in their time of need. God wants everyone to come to Him and He wants us to spread the news.

Praise is a powerful weapon against the enemy.

The devil hates to hear praise and worship coming out of your mouth. He is powerless against it. Praise defeats the ENEMY. What is your enemy? What do you fear, worry about, or dread? What do you fail at consistently? What are you addicted to? Instead of complaining about it, start praising God so you will remember that God is victorious. The enemy will hear you and learn that he has no chance against you.

Praise with the Word Of God

Use a Psalm or other Bible verse to praise God. For example, Psalm 46:1 "God is our refuge and our strength, an ever-present help in distress." Praise God now, using this small passage of scripture. Say out loud, "Father, you are my ever-present help in time of need." You are praising God with His word. Both Praise and the Word of God are powerful weapons against evil forces. The Bible describes the word of God as the SWORD OF THE SPIRIT.

> **Ephesians 6:16-17** *"In all circumstances, hold faith as a shield, to quench all [the] flaming arrows of the evil one. And take the helmet of salvation and the sword of the Spirit, which is the word of God."*

Let the Word of God come out of your mouth in the form of praise as often as you can or are willing. Are you moody? Begin praising God. Are you nervous? Begin praising God and see the enemy flee. The Bible says "So submit yourselves to God. Resist the devil, and he will flee from you" (James 4:7).

> **Psalm 66: 2-4** *"Shout joyful praises to God, all the earth! Sing about the glory of His name! Tell the world how glorious He is. Say to God, "How awesome are Your deeds! Your enemies cringe before Your mighty power. Everything on earth will worship You; they will sing Your praises, shouting Your name in glorious songs."*

> **Psalm 95:1-3** *"Come, let us sing for joy to the LORD; let us shout aloud to the rock of our salvation. Let us come before Him with thanksgiving and extol Him with music and song. For the LORD is the great God, the great King above all gods."*

> **Psalm 96:2-3** *"Sing to the Lord, bless His name; proclaim His salvation day after day. Tell His glory among the nations; among all peoples, his marvelous deeds."*

Notice it says, "SHOUT." Don't be shy. You have only just begun to praise God. Let's start by singing out loud and maybe raising our hands. Maybe we then begin to clap and even shout. God is worth it. You have to start somewhere, but start. Think about how much praise and attention we give the football player or singer.

Why do we praise God?

Praise honors God and we, His people, want to honor Him. When we praise God, we are letting God Himself know, and everyone on earth and under the earth know, who we believe in and honor as our Lord. We praise God because He is worthy of all honor and glory and praise.

> **Psalm 145:3** *"Great is the Lord and worthy of much praise, whose grandeur is beyond understanding."*

When we declare God as King of heaven and earth, we are not only obeying the Scripture that tells us to, but we are proclaiming ourselves His children at the same time. When we declare Him as our king, we are announcing that there is a kingdom and we are part of it. When we claim Jesus as our King, as God demands, we become part of that KINGDOM and live under His rule and protection, and all is ours. It is ours through our declaration. We don't sign a document or join a church to become a member of God's kingdom. We are born into it through the saving power of the blood of Jesus through our very own words, which demonstrate our heart.

> **Romans 10:8-10** *"But what does it say? "The word is near you, in your mouth and in your heart" (that is, the word of faith that we preach), for, if you confess with your mouth that Jesus*

is Lord and believe in your heart that God raised him from the dead, you will be saved. For one believes with the heart and so is justified, and one confesses with the mouth and so is saved."

Psalm 96:13 *"He governs the world with justice and the peoples with faithfulness."*

When we realize just how much God has done for us, we can't help but praise Him. We want the whole world to know. We don't want to keep it a secret.

Psalm 50:23 *"Those who offer praise as a sacrifice honor me."*

Hebrews 13:15 *"Through Jesus, therefore, let us continually offer to God a sacrifice of praise, the fruit of lips that openly profess His name."*

Psalm 138:2 *"I praise Your name for Your mercy and faithfulness. For You have exalted over all Your name and Your promise."*

Why do we praise God? (See verses from Psalm 145 below.)

Psalm 145

- **Verse 8** - The Lord is gracious and merciful, slow to anger and abounding in mercy.
- **Verse 9** - The Lord is good to all; compassionate toward all your works.
- **Verse 16** - The Lord satisfies the desire of every living thing.
- **Verse 17** - The Lord is just in all His ways. The Lord is merciful in all His works
- **Verse 18** - The Lord is near to all who call upon Him, to all who call upon Him in truth.

- **Verse 19** - The Lord fulfills the desire of those who fear Him. The Lord hears their cry and saves them.
- **Verse 20** - The Lord watches over all who love Him.

How Do We Praise God?

The Holy Spirit shows us how to praise. Praise is fruit of the outpouring of the Holy Spirit. Praise is a commitment, something we do on purpose. We praise God with our words, our instruments, our actions, our posture, our countenance, and with our love.

P Physical, clapping, raising hands. Praise should be evident.

R Raising hands as a gesture

A Anytime, anywhere, always

I Intentional

S Song

E Expressed

Psalm 66:8 says to let His praises be heard. Praise is not "praise" until it is vocalized. You can't praise your husband or your children by thinking about it. They just won't get the benefit until you actually say it. For some reason, it is easier to criticize than to applaud or express admiration and approval. Praising God does not come naturally to us but complaining does. We have to work at praise; it takes practice, commitment, and discipline.

Psalm 98:4-6 *"Shout with joy to the Lord, all the earth; break into song; sing praise. Sing praise to the Lord with the lyre, with the lyre and melodious song. With trumpets and the sound of the horn shout with joy to the King, the Lord."*

Psalm 138:2 *"I bow low toward your holy temple."*

Psalm 145:2 *"Every day I will bless you; I will praise your name forever and ever."*

Psalm 149:3 *"Let them praise His name with dancing; Let them sing praises to Him with timbral and lyre."*

Psalm 47:1 or 2 *"Come, everyone! Clap your hands! Shout to God wit h joyful praise!"*

Psalm 141:2 *"Let my prayer be incense before you; my uplifted hands an evening offering."*

Chronicles 20:18 "Then King Jehoshaphat bowed low, with his face touching the ground, and all the people bowed with him and worshiped the Lord."

When your words fail, praise God in tongues. Let the Holy Spirit praise through you.

Romans 8:26-27 *"In the same way, the Spirit too comes to the aid of our weakness; for we do not know how to pray as we ought, but the Spirit itself intercedes with inexpressible groanings. [27] And the one who searches hearts knows what is the intention of the Spirit, because it intercedes for the holy ones according to God's will."*

An excerpt from Pam Criss' teaching on GLORY AND PRAISE

"When we praise God with our voice, our mind will follow. It's hard to stay down when you are singing about how great your God is. Try it. Try repeating the following words of praise and see.

'God, you are all powerful, ever-living and ever-loving. You are God of all gods and Lord of all lords. You are the everlasting God, the maker of heaven and earth. Nothing is too difficult for you.' How do we give God the Glory He deserves? Truthfully, I don't think we ever can, but I believe we should die trying."

WHAT IS GLORY?

Psalm 29:1 and 2 "Give to the Lord, you heavenly beings, give to the Lord glory and might; Give to the Lord the glory due God's name. Bow down before the Lord's holy splendor."

Webster defines GLORY as very great praise, honor, or distinction bestowed by common consent. Also, adoring praise or worshipful thanksgiving. Another way to define GLORY is to give credit where credit is due.

A worldly example that I think we can all relate to is if someone makes a game winning shot at a basketball game, that person often gets the glory for winning the game. And how easy that is for us, to give a basketball player GLORY? Giving God the due Glory or praise He deserves should come naturally to us, but it often goes against what we learn in this world, which is too often self-centered and material. I believe the key to giving God glory, or giving God praise, is we have to ASK God for what we want and need so that He has the opportunity to answer us, and then we can give Him the glory and praise He deserves.

We don't like asking. We think for some reason we are bothering God. Why is asking so important? When we ask for something

from God, and He gives it to us or He does it, we can tell
everyone all about it. Then God gets all the glory. **Pam Criss**

When Do We Praise God?

- Always and forever.
- When it feels good and when it doesn't.
- When we feel like it and when we don't.
- In good times and in bad.
- Morning, noon and night.

> **2 Chronicles 20:22** *"As they began to sing and praise, the Lord*
> *set ambushes against the men of Ammon and Moab and Mount*
> *Seir who were invading Judah, and they were defeated."*

In 2 Chronicles, King Jehoshaphat fought the armies
coming against him with praise and worship. Joshua
conquered Jericho with a shout. Joshua and his armies
walked around the city praising God, and with one shout
the walls around the city fell (Joshua 6:20). God is trying to
tell us something. **He wages war differently.** Let's learn to
praise God. The Lord commands us to praise Him because
our praise has the power to defeat the enemy (see **Psalm
66:1–4** and **Psalm 145:1–4**).

I don't think THERE IS anything more pleasing to GOD
than to hear HIS PEOPLE SINGING PRAISE TO HIM,
especially as one body. God loves to hear you sing to Him.
God loves to hear us praise Him. Do you want to make God
happy? Start praising Him. Do you want to see the
atmosphere around you change? Start praising God. If you
don't know how to or what to say, start with the Psalms

listed below or the Praise Statements or the Litany of Praise in the following pages.

When we praise God, we are telling Him we understand who He is and what He has done for us. Our praise shows God our devotion, love, and trust in His power and goodness, and His desire to save, protect, and take care of us. We show Him we believe and accept His LORDSHIP! It's a huge factor. When we praise God for who He is and for what He has done, we prove to God we know what He has done and who He is. When I think of what Jesus did for me, I can't help but praise His holy name.

> **Psalm 95:1–3** *"Come, let us sing for joy to the LORD; let us shout aloud to the rock of our salvation. Let us come before Him with thanksgiving and extol Him with music and song. For the LORD is the great God, the great King above all gods."*

> **Psalm 150:1–6** *"Hallelujah! Praise God in His holy sanctuary; give praise in the mighty dome of heaven. Give praise for His mighty deeds, praise Him for His great majesty. Give praise with blasts upon the horn, praise Him with harp and lyre. Give praise with tambourines and dance, praise Him with strings and pipes. Give praise with crashing cymbals, praise Him with sounding cymbals. Let everything that has breath give praise to the LORD! Hallelujah!*

28

PRAISE AS A SACRIFICE

Psalm 50:14 *"Offer praise as your sacrifice to God; fulfill your vows to the Most High."*

Psalm 50:23 *"Those who offer praise as a sacrifice honor Me."*

S acrifice means giving something you treasure or prize for the sake of a higher calling. Sacrifice is something we do for the Lord. We do it just because He is Lord. Sacrifice is something we offer up. My mother used to tell us all the time, "Offer it up," referring to something we had to do that we didn't really want to do. When you offer something up for the sake of another, you do it whether you feel like it or not.

When we bring a sacrifice of praise to our Lord Jesus (in the form of song or dance or clapping or telling someone about Him), we are telling Him that He is worth our praise and worship, whether we feel like it or not. How much more do you think He appreciates us and our efforts when we do it even when we don't want to or when we don't feel like it?

God notices when we praise even though we might look foolish, or our voices are pitiful and off key.

> **Hebrews 13:15** *"Through Jesus, therefore, let us continually offer to God a sacrifice of praise — the fruit of lips that openly profess his name."*

This is what we do when we sing praises. In the Old Testament, the Hebrews offered sacrifices of bulls, goats, calves, grain, and the first fruits of the harvest. They offered their best, the unblemished lambs. The Lord tells us to praise Him with song and with music over and over in the Bible. Let's do it and let's give Him our best. He is worth our time, our effort, and our attention.

The devil hates it when we praise God.

In the Appendix, I am including my list of praise starters titled, "Praise Statements," as well as the "Litany of Praise" and "Daily Proclamations", and lastly my "Prayer of Commitment" and "Prayer of Surrender."

29

FINALLY

May this be the beginning of a new, successful, bold, and confident you. May you rise up out of every pit you have fallen into, crawled into, or were pushed into. You have the Greater One living in you so nothing is impossible for you. May your eyes be opened, and may your heart be receptive to the Word of God like never before. May you hunger for it and crave it more than anything the world has to offer. May His love overwhelm you and may the Holy Spirit reveal the Lord of Lords to you in a mighty and personal way. I pray that no weapon comes against you and every stronghold be broken in the name of Jesus.

God wants you more than you know and He has more gifts for you than you can possibly imagine or contain. I believe when we get to heaven, we will see a storehouse full of gifts bearing our name; gifts that were never opened. I heard a story once about a man who scheduled a trip from Europe to America.

Jack secured passage across the Atlantic, and while on the trip he remained in his cabin most of the time and brought with him snacks to hold him until he arrived. When he did venture out of his cabin, he saw men and women enjoying all that the ship offered, such as music, games, and dinners that to him looked like feasts. He was practically starving, but all he could do was watch. When the ship finally pulled into harbor in New York, he said in passing, to a fellow passenger, "It's a good thing we are here, I haven't eaten in days." The man looked at him incredulously. "Why not?" the fellow passenger said. The man said, "I brought only a few coins and could not afford the meals." The passenger replied, "Sir, the meals were included in the price of the passage."

Are you missing out on what is yours? Jesus did it all. He secured for you a place in heaven, but not only that, much, much more. You are seated at the Captain's table. Don't miss out on the meal plan that has already been provided. Jesus provided you with life, health, wholeness, peace, joy, liberty, and security here on earth, not just one day in heaven. His kingdom is here. Jesus said, "Thy kingdom come; thy will be done, on earth as it is heaven."

Don't miss this wonderful time we have on earth to thrive and live in Christ and for Him. Glorify the Lord with me, the Psalms encourage. Tell of His mighty deeds. What deeds can you tell others? What have you seen God do for you that you want to talk about to others? ASK and receive. You have no testimony because you have not yet asked in faith. Ask, God says, and you WILL receive. Open wide your hand and receive his goodness and then pass it on.

DAILY PROCLAMATIONS

Say any or all of these daily. These are declarations of faith. SPEAK and change your thoughts. Speak and cancel lies you have been listening to and believing. We are declaring what does not exist and calling it into being with our declarations.

> **Romans 4:17** *He is our father in the sight of God, in whom he believed, who gives life to the dead and calls into being what does not exist.*

We are declaring what does not exist and calling it into being. We do this because we have faith. We have faith that God is hearing and answering our prayers. Declaring is showing God we believe he heard our prayers. This is an excerpt written by Kate Johnston on declaring in faith.

> *"Declaring - Calling into being what does not exist." This is a huge statement (Romans 4:14). When I first read it, I didn't understand what it meant. But when I broke it down, I could see what an important statement this really is. HOW can you*

tell your husband, "You're the best," or, "I love you totally until the day I die," or, "I couldn't have chosen a better husband or father than you," how can you say this when you don't FEEL that way at the time? And that's the point, we do not have to FEEL, but just BELIEVE with eyes of faith. We can declare what is not, because we're standing on His promise. We're standing on His word believing that He is fighting for us, He is doing a work in our husbands that we don't see. He is fighting our battles. We are BELIEVING in that promise. BELIEVE when you don't see... that's FAITH.

Kate Johnston

COMMAND YOUR THOUGHTS

I command my thoughts into obedience. I put my mind on God. My mind is my property and mine to direct. I command every thought into obedience. Jesus, you are Lord of my mind, my thoughts, and my emotions. I give my mind to you. I trust you. I choose to think on your thoughts. I come against any thought that is not of you. I reject all evil thoughts and imaginations in the name of Jesus. Holy Spirit, give me discernment regarding thoughts. Let no weapon formed against me in my mind prosper against me. No thought will accuse me. No thought will threaten or lie to me. I choose to believe God and His word over the word of the accuser.

PHIL 4:8

"Finally, brothers, whatever is true, whatever is honorable, whatever is just, whatever is pure, whatever is lovely, whatever is gracious, if there is any excellence and if there is anything worthy of praise, think about these things."

DECLARE WHO YOU ARE

I am valuable; I am special to God. I have great worth, and my worth is not based on what others think of me, nor does it depend on what I accomplish or how I perform. Jesus Christ Himself gave His life for me and placed great value on me. I am deeply loved, pleasing, totally accepted and forgiven, and free, brand new, complete and whole in Christ.

DECLARING YOUR ALLEGIANCE AND HOPE

Jesus, I trust You. You care for me, and You care about me. You are for me and not against me. You know me, my every thought and my motives, and still You love me with a love that will never change. I am yours, and I am safe. Nothing can hurt me. You are my ever-present help in time of need. I run to you. I am yours and you will never desert me or fail me. You will never disappoint me. I will not doubt but trust in you.

IN TIMES OF FATIGUE AND WEARINESS

I will run and not grow weary; I will walk and not be faint. My future is secure. You have a plan in mind for me and a future full of hope. I will not fear or worry, but I choose to trust You with my life and my future. I am strong in the Lord and in His mighty Power. I can do all things through Christ who strengthens me. I am more than a conqueror through Him who loves me. I can overcome anything because Jesus will never leave me. He loves me just the way I am.

DECLARATION OF HEALING

Jesus, I am well. Your word says, "By Your wounds, I am healed." I receive your love and healing and thank You for doing that for me. Sickness and disease, my God, is greater.

My God is stronger, and my God is higher than you or anything you can throw at me. My God is my healer, awesome in power, and nothing is too difficult for Him. Psalm 103 says you forgive all my sins and heal all my diseases. I choose to believe it and I am counting on your word more than the thoughts of fear and doubt the enemy sends my way.

Jesus, You took my sins, sickness, and disease to the cross. I accept this gift and believe it is mine. I choose to walk by faith and not by sight. I choose to believe You are healing me now, no matter what it feels like. Your word says that You took our infirmities with You to the cross, and it says that You bore our diseases. I know You did that for me. Faith is not believing "God can," but that "God will." I believe I am healed. Lord help me with my unbelief.

The following may take more faith than you have right now. Say it anyway. Watch your faith grow as you trust God with your spouse.

SAY THESE DECLARATIONS OUT LOUD ...

FOR MY HUSBAND

My husband is a man after God's own heart. My husband loves me; he is selfless, content, generous, loving, and kind. My husband puts his wife and children first. My husband is God's problem, not mine. My husband is faithful and true. He is trustworthy. He is a good husband, and we are one in mind, body, and spirit. I love him and choose him.

FOR MY WIFE

My wife is a woman of God. My wife loves me, thinks about me, and cares for me. She is loving and kind. She puts me and the children first. I love her and will cherish her all the days of my life. She is my wife forever. She loves me and wants only the best for me. She is hard working, trustworthy, patient and kind. She is a good wife and we are one in mind, body, and spirit. I love her and choose her.

TO OVERCOME DEPRESSION

I come against you, depression, in the name of the Lord Almighty, in the name of Jesus whom you have defied. This day the Lord will deliver you, depression, into my hands, and I will strike you down and cut off your head. This very day I will give the carcass of depression to the birds and the wild animals, and the whole world will know that there is a God. I am a child of God and depression is not my lot in life. Jesus came to give me life and have it more abundantly. I am not depressed, I am filled with the Holy Spirit and life. I am rising up and walking and living today and every day. These symptoms will not get me down nor conquer me. I am more than a conqueror through Christ who strengthens me. I can do all things in Christ.

PSALM 18

"The LORD is my rock, my fortress and my deliverer; my God is my rock, in whom I take refuge, my shield and the horn of my salvation, my stronghold. I called to the LORD, who is worthy of praise, and I have been saved from my enemies.

PRAISE STATEMENTS / SCRIPTURES

SAY THESE OUT LOUD as a way to express your praise to God. You may respond to each phrase with *"Praise you, Jesus"* or *"Thank you, Lord"* or however the Holy Spirit leads you.

You are the everlasting God, the creator of all things, the creator of the universe.

You are the ever-loving and ever-living God.

You are my hope and I trust You in everything and always.

You never let me down, I can count on You.

You never fail me. You are my Father who loves me.

You are dependable. I depend on You, Lord Jesus

You are faithful and true to your Word. My future is in Your hands, You promise me a future full of hope.

You promise that your children will not have to beg for bread so I trust You for my daily bread, both now and forever. I will not fear.

You never give up on me, You never grow tired of me. You never weary of me.

You are my provider, You supply all my needs.

You open wide your hand and satisfy the desire of every living thing

You pardon all my sins and heal all my diseases.

You, Lord, are king.

You are all powerful, nothing is too difficult for you. With You ALL THINGS are possible. Everything is possible for those who believe.

You are my ever-present help in time of need.

You are near to all who call upon you in truth. Justice and righteousness are the foundation of Your throne.

Lord, You are compassionate and gracious, slow to anger, abounding in love.

Your unfailing love is higher than the heavens. Your faithfulness reaches to the clouds.

You will never leave me nor forsake me.

You sustain the poor and give bread to the hungry satisfying me with the finest of wheat.

You heal the sick, sustain me on my sick bed and restore me to full health.

You raise the dead to life.

You, LORD, take delight in me; You crown the humble with victory.

You are my defender, my strong tower, my mighty fortress. No weapon formed against me can stand. I am more than a conqueror through You, Lord Jesus.

If God is for me, who can be against me? You are FOR ME. I will not fear.

You redeem my life from the pit and crown me with love and compassion.

You satisfy my desires with good things so that my youth is renewed like the eagle's.

You move mountains for me, Lord,

You move heaven and earth for me, Your child.

You do not treat me as my sins deserve or repay me according to my iniquities. For as high as the heavens are above the earth, so great is Your love for those who fear You. As far as the east is from the west, You have removed my transgressions from me. I am Your child, an heir in Your kingdom.

You are my great warrior. I never fight my battles alone. You are my armor, my shield, my great protection.

You come to the aid of the orphan and the widow and thwart the way of the wicked.

You are faithful forever, securing justice for the oppressed.

You give sight to the blind and raise up those who are bowed down.

You set the prisoners free, and heal the brokenhearted binding up their wounds.

You preserve my life and keep my feet from slipping.

You guard me and watch over me. You command your angels to protect me.

Truly my soul finds rest in God; my salvation comes from Him.

Truly He is my rock and my salvation;

He is my fortress and security, I will never be shaken.

You command the wind and the waves. You hush the storm to silence.

Lord you are the Balm of Gilead, my healer.

You are my strength, and my champion. I can do all things through You, Lord Jesus.

You are the way to the Father. I come boldly to the throne of grace because You bore my sins.

You bore my sins and carried my diseases. By Your stripes I am healed. I am free from sin because of the price You paid.

You took my shame and the penalty due me. I am forgiven, Jesus did not die in vain. I walk in confidence and victory because of Jesus.

You are the Font of all holiness. You are the living water. Rivers of living water flow out of me because the Holy Spirit lives in me. The same Spirit that raised Jesus from the dead lives in me.

Jesus, You came to destroy the works of the devil. You are my deliverer. You deliver me from every evil.

You are the vine, we are the branches, without You I can do nothing.

Jesus, You are the Bread of Life, my sustenance.

You are my safety, my refuge, my God in whom I trust.

You deliver me from all my fears and save me from all my troubles.

Though the earth be shaken and the mountains quake, though the waters rage and foam and the mountains fall, I do not fear. The Lord of Hosts is with me.

Praise be to God, who has not rejected my prayer or withheld His love from me.

Lord I trust you completely because you are trustworthy.

You are the author of life, in You I live, move, and have my being.

You are the Alpha and the Omega, the first and the last, the beginning and the end.

You are the King of Kings, and Lord of all Lords. The great King over all God's. The Great I am.

You are my Lord, my God and my King. Amen

LITANY OF PRAISE

Recite with me and respond, "Praise you Jesus" after each phrase or whenever you would like .

Praise You, Jesus, You are my life, my love.

You are the name above all names.

You are Emmanuel, God with us.

You are the King of Kings.

You are the King of creation.

You are King of the universe.

You are the Lord of Lords.

Praise You, Jesus, You are the Almighty.

Praise You, Jesus, You are the Christ, Christ the King.

Praise You, Jesus, You are the Lamb of God.

Praise You, Jesus, You are Lion of Judah.

Praise You, Jesus, You are the Bright Morning Star.

Praise You, Jesus, You are our Champion and Shield.

Praise You, Jesus, You are our Strength and our Song.

Praise You, Jesus, You are the way of our life.

Praise You, Jesus, You are the only truth.

Praise You, Jesus, You are the real life.

Praise You, Jesus, You are the Wonderful Counselor.

Praise You, Jesus, You are the Prince of Peace.

Praise You, Jesus, You are the Light of the World.

Praise You, Jesus, You are the Living Word.

Praise You, Jesus, You are the Redeemer.

Praise You, Jesus, You are the Anointed One.

Praise You, Jesus, You are the Holy One of Israel.

Praise You, Jesus, You are the Good Shepherd.

Praise You, Jesus, You are the sheep gate.

Praise You, Jesus, You are the Lord of Hosts.

Praise You, Jesus, You are the Rock of all Ages.

Praise You, Jesus, You are my hiding place.

Praise You, Jesus, You are the Savior of the World.

Praise You, Jesus, You are the strong tower.

Praise You, Jesus, You are the mountain refuge.

Praise You, Jesus, You are the Bread of Life.

Praise You, Jesus, You are the Font of all Holiness.

Praise You, Jesus, You are the Living Water.

Praise You, Jesus, You are the True Vine.

Praise You, Jesus, You are my Spouse, my Maker.

Praise You, Jesus, You are our Fortress.

Praise You, Jesus, You are the Deliverer.

Praise You, Jesus, You are our Victory.

Praise You, Jesus, You are our Salvation.

Praise You, Jesus, You are our Righteousness.

Praise You, Jesus, You are our Wisdom.

Praise You, Jesus, You are our Sanctification.

Praise You, Jesus, You are our Justification.

Praise You, Jesus, You are the Door.

Praise You, Jesus, You are the great I AM.

Praise You, Jesus, You are the great High Priest.

Praise You, Jesus, You are the Cornerstone.

Praise You, Jesus, You are the Sure Foundation.

Praise You, Jesus, You are our Joy, our Portion and Cup.

Praise You, Jesus, You are my Healing and Wholeness.

Praise You, Jesus, You are our Covenant.

Praise You, Jesus, You are the Promise of the Father.

Praise You, Jesus, You are the Everlasting One.

Praise You, Jesus, You are the Most High God.

Praise You, Jesus, You are the Lamb that was slain.

Praise You, Jesus, You are the Just Judge.

Praise You, Jesus, You are the Balm of Gilead.

Praise You, Jesus, You are the Mighty Warrior.

Praise You, Jesus, You are my Defense.

Praise You, Jesus, You are the Bridegroom.

Praise You, Jesus, You are my Patience.

Praise You, Jesus, You are the Solid Reality

Praise You, Jesus, You are my Provider.

Praise You, Jesus, You are the Resurrection and the Life.

Praise You, Jesus, You are the Alpha and the Omega.

Praise You, Jesus, You are the Beginning and the End.

Praise You, Jesus, You are all that I need and all that I want.

Praise You, Jesus, You are worthy of all praise.

Amen

PRAYER OF COMMITMENT

God is not an option but an absolute necessity now! Don't wait! We can't live without Him. Without Him, we will live unfulfilling self-centered lives that are meaningless. He made us to live in communion with Him, and without Him, we are ruled by what others think of us. Choose Christ now TODAY and LIVE. Jesus gave it all for us and He stands at the door and knocks.

Prayer Of Commitment

"Dear Jesus, I believe You are the son of God and I believe You came to earth to die for me and to cleanse me of all my sins, guilt, and shame, and rose from the dead to bring me new life. You did this for me and You want me with you right now. Here I am, Lord, I want to belong to You from now on. Forgive me and free me from all darkness and evil, heal me and transform me into Your disciple. Thank You for loving me just the way I am. Because of You I can now say with confidence "I am forgiven; I am in Christ; and I am brand new. Amen."

PRAYER OF SURRENDER

Today I surrender to You, Lord Jesus. I surrender to You
because I trust You. I surrender all to You, my health, my
family, my finances, my work, my relationships, my
successes, and failures. I release it all to You. I surrender to
You, Lord, my fears, my insecurities, the past, the present,
and the future. I belong to You.

TO ORDER MORE BOOKS GO TO

https://www.spiritfilledcatholic.com/your-thoughts-are-killing-you
or email
mbwuenschel@gmail.com

ACKNOWLEDGMENTS

Tami Munsell - For believing in me from the start and for publishing and printing my first edition in 2012 at no cost to me.

Mehrak Ayati - For being my dearest friend, scrum master and the smartest woman I have every known. Thankful for your faith in me and for forcing me to believe in me.

Maria Chladny - For being there for me through thick and thin. My friend who is closer than a sister and confidant. I always know I can count on you.

Kate Johnston - For being a partner and friend and for co-leading retreats and "prayer breakfasts" with me. We have worked together so long, I can't imagine ministry without you.

Sheila Lovelace - For painstakingly going through the entire manuscript for my sake and for the sake of His Kingdom.

Debbie Fischange - For your support and for proofreading every chapter for me. Thank you for your sacrifice and diligence.

Pat Fischer - For proofreading, moral support and encouragement throughout this process.

Rhea Shoop, Judi Klausmeyer, Kim Healy, Kelly and Chris Fischer - My brother and sisters - For encouraging me to GO FOR IT.

Karen McCullough and Terry Svat - For your moral support and out of the box vision.

My Coach Marcy Pusey at SPS Publishing School for giving me the tools to succeed.

Made in United States
North Haven, CT
23 October 2023

43087525R00134